# Walk!
# Brittany (North)

*with*

*Charles Davis*

**DISCOVERY WALKING GUIDES LTD**

# Walk! Brittany (North)

First published June 2008

**Published by**
**Discovery Walking Guides Ltd**
10 Tennyson Close, Northampton NN5 7HJ,
England

**Maps**
Original 1:25,000 scale mapping is reproduced
under licence from Institut Geographique National,
Paris France.
Autorisation de Reproduction N° 41.0740

**Photographs**
Photographs in this book were taken by the author,
Charles Davis, and Jeanette Tallegas.

**Front Cover Photographs**

Walk 24 (Erquy)

Walk 40 (Fougeres)

Walk 23 (Hillion)     Walk 22 (Pordic: Cliffs & Coves)

ISBN 9781904946359

# Walk! Brittany (North)
## CONTENTS

## THE WALKS

### FINISTERE

#### COASTAL WALKS & ESTUARIES

## INLAND ITINERARIES

## CÔTES D'ARMOR

## COASTAL WALKS & ESTUARIES

## ILLE ET VILAINE

### COASTAL WALKS & ESTUARIES

### INLAND WALKS

# THE AUTHOR

Charles Davis was born in London, and has lived and worked in the United States, Sudan, Turkey, Ivory Coast, Spain and France. With the onset of middle age, he realised that the urge to roam was better satisfied by walking than bouncing about on the back of a lorry in the middle of the desert, and now divides his time between mountain tops, desk-tops and laptops. His first novel is being published in August 2007.

Jeanette Tallegas has spent thirty odd years labouring for the French education system, from which she has finally, gleefully, taken early retirement. Asked what she intends doing now, she resolutely replies, "Nothing". Nonetheless, she does follow the author up various gruelling mountains, frequently alarming younger walkers who seem to assume that remote and inaccessible places are the preserve of youth.

Charles Davis is also the author of:-

Walk! The Alpujarras — ISBN 9781904946236

Walk! Mallorca (North & Mountains) (2nd Edition) — ISBN 9781904946199

Walk! Mallorca West — ISBN 9781899554980

Walk! La Gomera — ISBN 9781899554904

Walk! La Palma — ISBN 9781904946069

Walk! Andorraa — ISBN 9781904946045

Walk! Axarquía — ISBN 9781904946083

Walk! The Lake District South — ISBN 9781904946168

Walk! Dorset — ISBN 9781904946205

- published by **Discovery Walking Guides Ltd.**

## TO THE ENDS OF THE EARTH

Brittany is France's Celtic fringe, bearing the same topographical relationship to the rest of the country as Cornwall does to Britain, and an emotional, political and historical link comparable to that of Scotland and Wales with England. One might even call it a fringe beyond the fringe, because it was to Brittany that the residents of Britain's nascent Celtic fringe withdrew at the end of the Roman Empire when the Saxons got bothersome back home in Cornwall and Wales. In other words, Brittany is out on the edge of things, and for many years the rest of France was determined to keep it that way, except insofar as the peninsula was able to provide a steady supply of fish and cheap labour.

Nowadays Brittany is very much a part of modern France and is an increasingly fashionable domestic holiday destination for those who have tired of the crowded beaches and traffic jams that a traditional southbound break entails. Nonetheless, the old ways endure, Celtic culture is flourishing and is more vibrantly celebrated than ever before, and the region is highly recommended for anyone looking for an interesting break in a place that is at once French but something other, as well.

And something 'other' it is, too. A repository of sailors, domestic servants, *gendarmes*, and occasionally cannon-fodder, Brittany was in many ways France's first colony. In the days when bourgeois French families could afford domestic servants, *une bonne Bretonne* was an essential piece of equipment, and even those that couldn't afford one probably profited from the services of Breton labour, for the Bretons were the first and definitive migrant class, so much so that later immigrants were initially called *'Bretons noirs'*.

Yet, despite or possibly because of its vital role sustaining the economy, Brittany was traditionally treated by the nation at large as a sort of running joke, the residents of which were handy for the hands-on-work, endearing for their comical simplicity, but faintly dangerous and not exactly *comme il faut*.

To give you an idea of the region's reputation, the French word *plouc* is taken from the classic prefix of many Breton villages, and has much the same connotations as 'peasant' or 'bumpkin' in English. By the same token, Breton migrants are said to have introduced a new word into French vocabulary, *baragouin,* meaning 'gibberish' or 'jabber', taking its derivation from Breton speaking peasants turning up in Paris demanding bread and wine, *bara* and *guin*. Meanwhile, the Breton language itself was so heavily censured, children caught using it in the playground were shamed by having a clog hung round their neck, which they couldn't get rid of until they had in turn caught and denounced someone else, while public buildings like post-offices once had signs up saying it was forbidden to spit on the floor or speak Breton!

Yet despite being out on the edges and systematically marginalized, Brittany has played a pivotal role in defining France for foreign eyes. Breton sailors with a wife in every port probably did as much if not more to plant the seed of French culture abroad than any number of governmental committees. Breton explorers and privateers mapped out the emotional and geographical pattern of Imperial France. The Breton Johnnies, with their onion laden bikes, berets, stripy T-shirts and eternal maize paper fag, established for ever the stereotypical image of a Frenchman. And the most famous Frenchman in the world, Asterix the Gaul, came from the Breton village of **Erquy**.

Brittany is, therefore, a place of contradictions: lying at the ends of the earth and for many years deemed beyond the pale, it has been instrumental in the fashioning of French identity, at once defining and expanding frontiers, and exporting images of France around the world. Long despised by urbane sophisticates as a place in which people knew better how to park a cow than a car and dismissed by many French holidaymakers as one long wet shower, it is nowadays becoming dangerously fashionable as the urban sophisticates and holidaymakers, having endured one blistering heatwave too many, desperately scrabble about trying to buy a seaside home in Brittany. Look around when you arrive and you'll soon understand why. This maybe the end of the earth, but it's definitely a place you want to be.

## WALKING IN BRITTANY

Plage de Guen (Walk 24)

The best known and most obvious walking in Brittany is along the *sentier cotier* that snakes its way along the coast, and very fine it is, too. Beaten out by countless customs officers traipsing along the clifftops and round the coves in search of the smugglers for whom the rugged shoreline was a perfect embarkation point, it is one of the world's great coastal paths.

Weaving round spectacular estuaries, dipping into exquisite hidden creeks, skirting fabulous sandy beaches, flirting with crumbling cliffs, thundering up and down the relentless rollercoaster fashioned by millennia of erosion, ploughing through expansive sand dunes, detouring round wild headlands, traversing astonishing rockscapes, taking the rambler past placid turquoise seas as clear as the Western Med and within spitting distance of roiling turmoils of pounding surf…well, you get the idea, the *sentier cotier* has got the lot and offers hours of entertainment to dedicated hikers and casual tourists alike.

Walk 2, Trézien

Planning this book, it was hard to tear myself away from the coast, as it boasts so many great walks, I could easily have filled half a dozen volumes with purely coastal itineraries. But tear myself away I did and tear yourself away you must as there are some glorious walks in the hinterland, and any visitor who restricted themselves to the coast would only have a very partial perspective on the region. Admittedly, it would be partial in every sense of the term, at once limited and favourably biased, but still, I strongly recommend making the effort to go further afield than that first frontier.

Walk 10, Plougasnou

Despite a regrettable tradition of intensive pig farming, the Breton hinterland is for the most part an unspoiled pastoral landscape of irregular higgledy-piggledy fields and low rolling hills. Dotted with delightful villages and lovely hamlets, many with astonishingly elaborate churches and chapels, it's a landscape that has not quite escaped time, but has at least hindered its progress.

Fields are still defined by embankments and hedgerows and patched with coppicing, while the hills are interleaved with lovely wooded valleys, winding rivers, hidden lakes, secluded streams and, that most Breton of topographical features, the *chaos*, a cataract

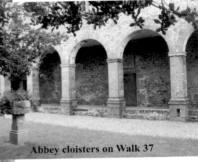
Abbey cloisters on Walk 37

of great granite boulders polished by water erosion, and clad in woodland so dense and tangled it often aspires to a tropical fecundity.

The principal woods of Brittany are composed largely of chestnut and oak, but there are plenty of beech, birch and ash, too, while the colonizing commercial pine rarely supplant the indigenous broadleaf trees.

Huelgoat forest (Walks 15 & 16)

The most famous forests are **Huelgoat** and **Paimpont**, respectively the western and eastern remnants of the woodland that once covered the Breton interior, and which was later identified with the Broceliande forest of Arthurian romance. **Paimpont** does not feature in the present volume due to restricted access during the hunting season, but there are two itineraries in **Huelgoat** and several others featuring extensive woodland walking.

Heath or moorland is another characteristic, both inland and on the coast, and many seaside walks feature an aesthetically pleasing combination of clifftop, heath and beach, albeit with a bit of tarmac generally proving inevitable if we want to do a loop rather than a simple there and back linear itinerary.

There are also some attractive little hummocky things that the Bretons are pleased to call 'mountains'. Best not to make an issue of this. It's a "don't mention the war" thing really. The Bretons are very fond of their mountains (if challenged, they will defensively tell you they are 'old' mountains) and, despite the fact that none of the said mountains tops the statutory 600-metre definition (they don't even make 400 metres!), it's best to humour the locals. Just nod your head and smile and say yes. It doesn't really matter. These 'mountains' are, after all, very nice places with lots of nice walks. But they are undeniably small. It's a bit like calling Richmond Park a prairie or saying a Chihuahua is a kind of wolf. Certain defining characteristics are discernible, but the essential dimension of the thing is missing.

As a general rule, walking in Brittany is a relatively gentle affair, but for those who like their walking on the energetic side, there are enough lung-busting rollercoasters on the *sentier cotier* to keep you puffing and perspiring, walks that can seem much tougher than bigger climbs elsewhere due their unremitting ups and downs.

## PRACTICALITIES

The **focus** of the book is on the bit of Brittany that, for obvious reasons, the majority of British visitors reach first, for the most part via the ferry ports of **Saint Malo** and **Roscoff**, but increasingly on budget flights between Stanstead and Dinard, and Southampton and Brest.

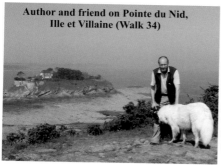

**Author and friend on Pointe du Nid, Ille et Villaine (Walk 34)**

For the sake of convenience, the **walks are divided** according to the administrative *departements* of **Finistére**, **Côtes d'Armor**, and **Ille et Villaine**, covering **Côtes d'Armor** in its entirety and the northern part of the other two.

The walks in each area are varied, but to give the first time visitor a rough idea, **Finistére** is the wild western land facing the Atlantic with plenty of rugged coastal walks, plus those 'mountains'; **Côtes d'Armor** boasts its own rugged coast and some fine estuaries, but also has a great selection of inland walks in the valleys and woods surrounding the picturesque villages that more and more English expats are discovering; **Ille et Villaine** meanwhile, due to its greater proximity to Paris, is the place where the tourist infrastructure is most developed, as a result of which we concentrate on itineraries off the beaten track in the forests and along the waterways away from the coast.

Within each section, the **walks are arranged** in a roughly geographical order from west to east, each itinerary being prefaced by the name of the nearest town or village for ease of location. As a rule, the walks tend to be longer than those featured in Discovery Walking Guides' more mountainous destinations, but short versions are cited where practical for people who don't fancy quite such a marathon.

The **best maps** are the French IGN's 1:25,000 blue map series, which are designed for walkers, cyclists and horse-riders. If you wish to explore a given area in more detail, they are available in newsagents and bookshops. It should be noted though that the maps appear to be based on aerial photography, as a consequence of which paths through woods often don't feature unless they're part of a recognized long distance trail, so it's worth inquiring in tourist offices for additional information that IGN haven't picked up on. Likewise for customary and permissive rights-of-way, only a small proportion of which are covered by IGN's red highlighted routes. You will also encounter differences on coastal itineraries where the GR34 and *sentier cotier* (which more or less correspond but occasionally diverge from one another) have changed route to mitigate erosion and the mapping has yet to catch up with realities on the ground.

Walks are preceded by our usual **rating guide,** summarizing exertion, time, distance, climbs, refreshments and access. Since very few of these walks simply set off from a base and climb steadily to a culminating point, the ascents and descents are generally estimated rather than precisely measured.

**Access** is rarely disputed and certainly shouldn't be a problem on any of the walks detailed here. As a rough guideline, France does not enjoy quite such an elaborate system of rights-of-way across agricultural land as Britain and there is as yet nothing comparable to the right-to-roam legislation. However, dirt tracks and traditional sunken paths are nearly always treated as rights-of-way and a huge amount of work has been done by local authorities negotiating fieldside rights of way linking established routes to create coherent itineraries.

The same joke about the **weather** is told in Brittany as in Wales. Tourist takes refuge from the rain in a bar and asks a local youth if it's been raining long. "I don't know", comes the reply, "I'm only eighteen". In fact, Brittany's reputation for rain is exaggerated. I'm told (somewhat improbably, it must be said) there's actually higher annual rainfall in Cannes than in Brest, and from personal experience associate the region with long, lazy, sunny summers awash with azure blue skies and turquoise seas. There's often a lovely Indian Summer in September after the tourists have gone and even mid-winter (notably January) can enjoy extended periods of crisp cold weather with deep blue skies. Even so, it's best to work on the Breton assumption that it's going to be fine 'several times a day'. Keep a light waterproof in your backpack at all times and wear walking shoes that can cope with a bit of mud. If you can follow French, it's worth consulting the official recorded forecast. Telephone 08-92-68-01 followed by the *departementale* number: 29 for Finistére, 22 for Côtes d'Armor, and 35 for Ille et Villaine.

3

our rating for effort/exertion:-
**1** very easy          **2** easy          **3** average
**4** energetic          **5** strenuous

approximate **time** to complete a walk (compare your times against ours early in a walk) - does not include stopping time

 8 km

approximate walking **distance** in kilometres

 200m  850m

approximate **ascents/descents** in metres (N = negligible)

**circular** route

**linear** route

**risk of vertigo**

**refreshments** (may be at start or end of a route only)

Walk descriptions include:
- timing in minutes, shown as (40M)
- compass directions, shown as (NW)
- GPS waypoints, shown as (Wp.3)

# MAP NOTES

The map sections used in this book have been taken from the 1:25,000 scale Blue Map series published by Institut Geographique National of Paris, France. Reproduction of the sections of these maps has been licensed from IGN-Paris under the 'Autorisation de Reproduction de Representation ou d'Adaption N° 41.0740'. Each map section includes the reference to the IGN map sheet from which it is taken, and the map sheets are also listed on pages 14 & 15.

IGN's Blue Map 25k series are widely available in France and are available through UK bookshops, though probably best to contact a map specialist such as Stanfords or The Map Shop (Upton upon Severn).

www.ign.fr is the official IGN website, with information available in English, giving more than enough information on their printed map products though, unfortunately, their digital mapping available on CD is sadly lacking in explanation and only in French.

## IGN MAP SHEETS

# Brittany

The GPS Waypoint lists provided in Walk! Brittany (North) guide book are as recorded by Charles Davis during his research of this book. In the interests of clarity not all waypoints in these lists are shown on the maps which accompany each detailed walk description. Where a Waypoint symbol is shown on a map it is placed alongside the position it refers to so as to not obscure the map detail and is numbered so that it can directly identified against the walk description and waypoint list.

GPS Waypoints are quoted for the WGS84 Datum and UTM Position Format, the same datum and position format as the IGN maps, so the Waypoints are also the Grid References for the IGN map sheets.

All The GPS Waypoints quoted are subject to the general considerations as to the accuracy of GPS units in the location concerned. Brittany generally has good GPS reception with the only reception problems you might encounter occurring in some of the denser woods.

Routes where you might encounter gps reception problems are:-

6. Mogueriec; some moderate interference in the more densely wooded areas.

15. Huelgoat; reasonable reception in dense woodland at the start but relatively poor amid the taller, more spacious trees after Squiriou.

23. Hillion; some interference in woods approaching Gouessant.

27. Belle Isle; poor reception in the woods, wpts 4&5 and again approaching wpt 10.

29. Tremargat; poor reception in gorge after wpt 20 and some interference from tree cover.

31. Ploufragan; poor reception in the woods at the start.

32. Langast; intermittent interference from tree cover.

38. St. Medard; poor reception in the densest stretches of the Bois de Cranne.

If you are using a Sirf chipset equipped gps unit you will probably experience better reception in these areas.

It is virtually impossible to reproduce the exact GPS Waypoint co-ordinates in practice when walking a route. In practice you should expect 10 metres as an acceptable standard of gps accuracy when you have '3D navigation' (four or more satellites in view); though reception is often good enough for your accuracy to be closer to 5 metres.

## Signal Strength

Signal strength from sufficient satellites is crucial to obtaining an accurate location fix with your GPS unit. In open sky conditions you may have up to 11 satellites in view to give you a GPS location accuracy of 5 metres. Providing you have good batteries, and wait until your GPS has full 'satellite acquisition' before starting out, your GPS will perform wonderfully in Brittany.

## To Input the Waypoints

GPS Waypoint co-ordinates are quoted for the WGS84 Datum in UTM Co-ordinates, used to provide grid references on the IGN maps.

To input the Waypoints into your GPS we suggest that you:
- switch on your GPS and select 'simulator' mode.
- check that your GPS is set to the WGS84 datum (its default datum) and the 'location format' 'UTM'. If you have been using your gps in UK then you

have probably set the Datum to OSGB and Location Format to BNG (British National Grid), it is most important that you set your gps to WGS84 Datum and UTM Location Format before inputting the Waypoints.

- input the GPS Waypoints into a 'route' file with the same number as the walking route number; then when you call up the 'gps route' in Brittany there will be no confusion as to which walking route it refers to.

- repeat the inputting of routes until you have covered all the routes you plan to walk, or until you have used up the memory capacity of your GPS; even the most basic of GPS units will store up to 20 routes of up to 50 Waypoints for each route, and you can always re-programme your GPS while in Brittany.

- turn off your GPS. When you turn the GPS back on it should return to its normal navigation mode.

GPS Waypoints are provided as an additional navigation aid to complement the detailed walk descriptions in Walk! Brittany (North). Knowing exactly where you are in relation to our detailed walk description is a great confidence booster when exploring these new and exciting landscapes. GPS Waypoints are provided for all key navigational points on all walking routes; never again should you find yourself wondering whether you are on the right path or not. Note that GPS Waypoints complement the detailed walking route descriptions, and are not intended as an alternative to those descriptions.

## Personal Navigator Files (PNFs) for Brittany

Full GPS Track and Waypoint records for the walking routes contained in Walk! Brittany (North) are available on DWG's Personal Navigator Files CD which also includes GPS Track and Waypoint files for our Abroad walking routes in the Alpujarras, Andorra, Sierra de Aracena, Tenerife, Lanzarote, La Gomera, La Palma, Mallorca (North & Mountains), Mallorca (West), Madeira, Menorca and our UK walking routes for Brecon Beacons, Devon, Dartmoor, Dorset, Exmoor, Isle of Wight, Lake District North, Lake District South, Peak District (South), South Downs, South Pennines, and Yorkshire Dales (North & Central).

In addition to the GPS Track and Waypoint Files our PNFs CD includes GPS Utility Special Edition software for loading the files to your gps unit, and Google Earth files for many of our walking routes. That's a 'lot of navigation' for £9.99 inc VAT and postage. See our websites for latest PNF information.

## Confused by GPS?

If you are confused by talk of GPS, but are interested in how this modern navigational aid could enhance your walking enjoyment then simply seek out a copy of GPS The Easy Way, the UK's best selling GPS manual. Written in an easy to read, lively, style and lavishly illustrated 'GPS The Easy Way' takes you through all aspects of GPS usage from absolute basics up to GPS Expert and debunking the myths about GPS along the way; an essential purchase for anyone thinking of buying a GPS.

GPS The Easy Way is available from bookshops, outdoor shops, over the Internet, and post free from Discovery Walking Guides Ltd.
www.walking.demon.co.uk & www.dwgwalking.co.uk

No question about it, the **Pointe de St. Mathieu** is one of Brittany's most dramatic and accessible headlands, dominating the entrance to the strategic anchorage of the **Rade de Brest**, and confronting everything (and it's a lot) that the Atlantic cares to chuck at this exposed coast. Slightly more questionable is the official title of the circuit round the headland, since the abbey that was once the defining manmade feature of the *pointe* has been treated with what one can only assume is a fine republican disdain for the sacred, a lighthouse and coastguard station having been planted in, around and between the abbey's ruins and its chapel. It certainly makes for a very striking image on what is already a very striking walk, combining two waymarked itineraries to explore a wonderfully wild stretch of coast sandwiched between the heavily cultivated plateau and the sea. It is very exposed, though, so consult the forecast first and go prepared.

\*there's only one stop en route, the hostellerie at the **Pointe St. Mathieu**, but it is perfectly located.

| Strolls | Short Version |
|---|---|
| If you don't feel like a full walk, it's definitely worth driving to the *pointe* and just pottering about the headland. | Either of the waymarked loops of which our itinerary is composed (see Wps. 7&20). |

**Access:** on foot from **Plougonvelin**

Our itinerary starts from the **Fort de Bertheaume** car park (signposted throughout **Plougonvelin**) (Wp.1 0M), from where we stroll back up the road leading to the village, passing the **Bertheaume** campsite. We then take the second turning on the left (Wp.2 7M), a residential road through the hamlet of **Keruzas**, which has long since been absorbed by the municipality of **Plougonvelin**.

At the crossroads to the west of **Keruzas**, we carry straight on (Wp.3 13M) along a dirt track leading to a metalled lane on the edge of the hamlet of **Poulherbet** (Wp.4 20M). Turning right then left 75 metres later (Wp.5), we continue on tarmac to the T-junction at **Keryunan** (Wp.6 29M), where we turn right then immediately left to pass the picturesque springs of the same name.

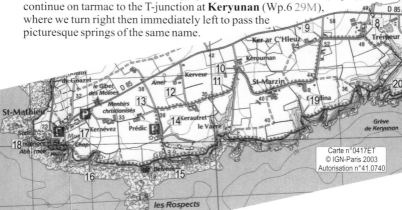

Carte n°0417ET
© IGN-Paris 2003
Autorisation n°41.0740

75 metres after an asphalted turning on the right, we leave the first of our combined loops, forking right (Wp.7 33M) on a dirt track leading to another lane in the hamlet of **Trémeur** (Wp.8 39M).

Bearing left, we follow this lane to a crossroads with another, broader lane, where we turn left (Wp.9 44M), staying on tarmac as we trace a long dogleg across the agricultural plateau around **St.Marzin**. As the lane approaches the D85, we double back to the left on a minor lane (Wp.10 58M) passing the lovely little *lavoir* (an open air washhouse) of **Poul ar C'holven**, which is currently being restored by local farmers.

**The lovely little *lavoir***

Immediately after the *lavoir* (a nice spot for a break on the outward leg; note the 'kneeling box' for protecting the washerwomen's skirts and the paddle for beating the clothes), we fork right on a dirt track beside a shallow stone trough (Wp.11 60M), crossing a lane beside a farmhouse 200 metres later (Wp.12 64M).

At the intersection with the next lane (Wp.13 67M), the old itinerary carrying straight on through the **Prédic** and **Kérnevez** farms is in the process of being suppressed, so we stick with the waymarked route, turning left to reach a long oval turning circle. At the tip of the turning circle (Wp.14 70M), a track curves off to the left toward a line of blockhouses and a grassy trail heads due south. We take the grassy trail, which soon joins the **GR34**/*sentier cotier* (Wp.15 73M). If time's short or the weather is really vile, simply turn left here to return to **Plougonvelin**. However, I strongly recommend visiting the headland itself. Quite apart from anything else, the *pointe* is even more spectacular in vile weather, besides which there's an unusual belvedere 100 metres later that provides adequate shelter against the elements.

Heading west, the GR joins a farm track that we follow to the left for 100 metres (Wp.16 84M) before turning left on the path (Wp.17) circling the lighthouse/abbey to reach the monument to sailors lost at sea (Wp.18 94M). We then circle round the cenotaph and retrace our steps to Wp.15 (111M),

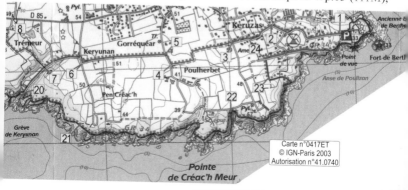

**Approaching the _pointe_**

from where we simply follow the coast path back to the start. This is well-waymarked and nearly always self-evident, so rather than making a bid for Champion Statement of the Obvious, I will simply summarize key points en route for the purpose of pacing progress.

- When the trail broadens to a grassy farm track, we turn right to stay on the coast path (Wp.19 131M).
- We cross the end of the road below Wp.7 (Wp.20 144M).
- At a wayposted Y-junction below 'Keryunan', we fork right for 'Bertheaume 3.6km' (Wp.21 155M).
- Just short of the access road to a red and white mast, we fork right (Wp.22 178M).
- The path eventually veers away from the coast (the old route was cut by a landslip and access is now completely overgrown) to a T-junction of tracks (Wp.23 190M) where we turn right then right again at the next T-junction (Wp.24 192M), after which we simply carry straight on to return to the carpark.

# 2 TRÉZIEN: POINTE DE CORSEN – BRETONS RULE THE WAVES

Following quiet country lanes in the hinterland and broad trails along the coast, the tour of the **Pointe de Corsen** is an ideal way to discover the Breton *sentier cotier*, rewarding the walker with high drama for minimal effort. Confronting the big Atlantic sky and oceanic swell, the low cliffs of crumbling rock are frequently rimed with surf and are punctuated by pretty little sandy beaches boasting fine views across outcrops of more resilient but still ragged rock toward the **Ouessant/Molène** archipelago. Historically though, this seascape has been regarded with rather more dread than aesthetic appreciation. The **Chenal du Four** dividing the islands from the mainland is a notoriously dangerous channel, fraught with strong currents and spattered with innumerable islets and reefs, on which countless mariners have come to grief. Our itinerary is an extended circuit around the hub of the CROSS (Centre Régional Opérationnel de Surveillance et de Sauvetage) command centre, which was established at **Trézien** after the sinking of the Amoco-Cadiz in 1978 to monitor maritime traffic along the northern and western coasts of Brittany, coordinate lifeboat and fishery operations, and implement anti-pollution measures. The coastguard probably don't precisely rule the waves, but if you happen to be here during a gale, you'll be glad they're at least keeping an eye on them. The sight of the waters working themselves up into a tizzy is enough to excite a lively sympathy with anyone at peril on the sea.

**Access:** on foot from **Trézien** (south-west of **Lampaul-Plouarzel**)

We set off from the car park immediately south of **Trézien** church and cemetery (Wp.1 0M), strolling back past the church into the village centre, where we turn right at the calvary (Wp.2 2M) then left a little over 100 metres later on the cheeringly named 'Rue de la Luronne' (Wp.3 4M) - which loosely translates as 'Gay Hussy Road'! At the end of 'Gay Hussy', we turn right (Wp.4 13M), then left at a T-junction in front of a small white house with blue shutters (Wp.5 16M), taking a 50-metre sliproad to reach one of the main lanes linking the coast with the hinterland (Wp.6). Descending to the left, we approach the beach of **Porz Tévigné**, where we again turn left on the sandy, picket fenced coastal path (Wp.7 25M).

The coastal path winds alongside low cliffs of crumbling rock, passing a second, small beach (Wp.8 38M) before crossing a road accessing a third beach (Wp.9 42M). N.B. 100 metres to the south of this waypoint, there's a very rudimentary but friendly and appealing little bar, the only refreshment en route (open on school holidays and at weekends out of season). 150 metres later, we can fork right if we wish (Wp.10 45M) following the line of the coast before rejoining the main path 25 metres later, within sight of the **Pointe de Corsen**.

Sticking with the trail defined by the ankle-high anti-erosion 'fences', we soon join a dirt track (Wp.11 55M), where we bear right, either along the track

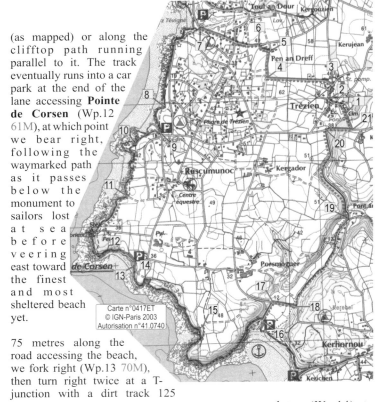

(as mapped) or along the clifftop path running parallel to it. The track eventually runs into a car park at the end of the lane accessing **Pointe de Corsen** (Wp.12 61M), at which point we bear right, following the waymarked path as it passes below the monument to sailors lost at sea before veering east toward the finest and most sheltered beach yet.

75 metres along the road accessing the beach, we fork right (Wp.13 70M), then turn right twice at a T-junction with a dirt track 125

**Looking back from Wp.13**

metres later (Wp.14) to continue on the coastal path. The path meanders across heathland overlooking less eroded cliffs, then, after a brief but steady little climb, runs into a track (Wp.15 85M), where we turn right to stay on the 'Sentier Cotier'. Eventually, we dip round a final headland and head NE toward the large **Porsmoguer** beach and dunes.

Emerging on a lane behind the beach's western car park (Wp.16 99M), we leave the GR and bear left, heading inland to the main coast road (Wp.17 101M). Turning right, then left 125 metres later (Wp.18 103M), we follow a broad grassy trail along the eastern flank of a delightful little valley. Our trail broadens to a track which is surfaced for the last couple of hundred metres as it approaches a major lane through the hamlet of **Pont ar Floc'h** (Wp.19 114M). Turning left, we follow this lane for 750 metres until we come to a T-junction, where we turn right (Wp.20 124M) then left 100 metres later (Wp.21) to return to **Trézien**.

# 3 PORTSALL: SHIPWRECKERS' RAPTURE

Often as not when reaching for a metaphor to describe the Breton coast, a writer will come up with something related to needlework, leastways I do and I don't think it's simply from a paucity of imagination. Hemming, stitching, embroidery all suggest themselves naturally. But if ever a shoreline merited a description based on the notion of something minutely worked by nimble fingers, it is this fabulous stretch of coast where the English Channel gives way to the Atlantic.

It's an extraordinary place, a long low line of higgledy piggledy rock braided and abraded by the indefatigable battering of the surf, while out to sea there are so many islets and rocks protruding from the waves, the agitated water looks like a bunch of brawling sheep. Little wonder then that peddlers of popular nineteenth century fictions located the largely imaginary activities of shipwreckers at this end of the peninsula. For anyone with evil in mind and lamp in hand, not to mention a pen and a publisher's deadline, this desolate windswept landscape provided all the heart could desire.

\* at **Portsall**

**Access:**
on foot from **Portsall**

### Strolls
The D127 runs parallel to the coastal path from **Penfoul** to Portsall, as a result of which every stretch of this fabulous coast can be reached by all but the most invincibly lethargic.

The walk starts from the southern end of **Port de Portsall** at the 'Square de l'Aberic' car-park, between the 'Crêperie La Chaumine' and the 'Restaurant les Littorines'. Setting off on a narrow drive signposted 'Allée Couverte Guilliguy' (Wp.1 0M), we follow the GR-waymarked footpath onto the **Pointe du Guilligui**. At the crossroads behind the calvary and dolmen (Wp.2), we carry straight on, then turn right at the end of a tarmac lane (Wp.3 5M) on a narrow path descending to the water's edge. After following a lane up to the D27, we turn right (Wp.4 8M) then immediately left (leaving the GR) on 'Rue de Prat an Eol' (Field of Wind Road!).

At the end of the lane, we turn left (Wp.5 11M) then right on 'Route de Viaduc' (Wp.6 14M) and cross the old railway viaduct, after which we carry straight on at three crossroads in quick succession (re-crossing the D27 at the last junction). As the tarmac lane swings right toward house N° 8, we again carry straight on, now following an attractive grassy dirt track intermittently lined with honeysuckle (Wp.7 22M). When the track joins another asphalted lane a little over a kilometre later (Wp.8 37M), we turn left, rejoining the D27 beside the 'Chez Pat' pizza-snack bar (Wp.9 40M).

Turning right, we follow the D27 for 600 metres, initially on the road itself, but soon alongside it on a well-trodden verge. The pedestrian way disappears at **Landunvez**, but 100 metres later (just before the end of speed limit sign),

**Pointe de Landunvez**

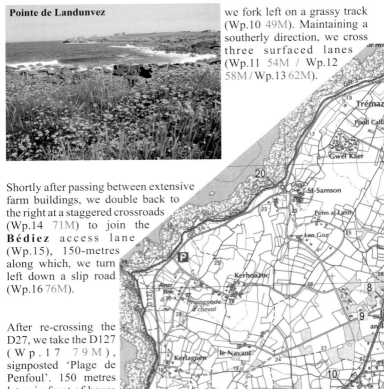

we fork left on a grassy track (Wp.10 49M). Maintaining a southerly direction, we cross three surfaced lanes (Wp.11 54M / Wp.12 58M / Wp.13 62M).

Shortly after passing between extensive farm buildings, we double back to the right at a staggered crossroads (Wp.14 71M) to join the **Bédiez** access lane (Wp.15), 150-metres along which, we turn left down a slip road (Wp.16 76M).

After re-crossing the D27, we take the D127 (Wp.17 79M), signposted 'Plage de Penfoul'. 150 metres later, in front of house N°6, we turn left, as indicated by GR waymarks (Wp.18 81M), on an unnamed lane leading to house N°15 (on our left) and the coastal path proper (Wp.19 84M).

Carte n°0417ET
© IGN-Paris 2003
Autorisation n°41.0740

**St. Samson**

There's no call for description until we get back to **Portsall** bay, as we now simply follow the superb coastal path, staying as near the water's edge as prudence and the ankle high cables protecting the vegetation permit. For the purposes of pacing progress, the principal landmark is the chapel and spring of **St. Samson** (Wp.20 121M), after which the chaos of rock and the roaring of the surf are generally a little calmer. Two kilometres later, we join a tarmac lane on the **Beg ar Galéti** headland (Wp.21 146M).

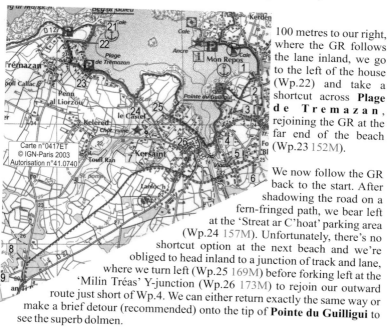

100 metres to our right, where the GR follows the lane inland, we go to the left of the house (Wp.22) and take a shortcut across **Plage de Tremazan**, rejoining the GR at the far end of the beach (Wp.23 152M).

We now follow the GR back to the start. After shadowing the road on a fern-fringed path, we bear left at the 'Streat ar C'hoat' parking area (Wp.24 157M). Unfortunately, there's no shortcut option at the next beach and we're obliged to head inland to a junction of track and lane, where we turn left (Wp.25 169M) before forking left at the 'Milin Tréas' Y-junction (Wp.26 173M) to rejoin our outward route just short of Wp.4. We can either return exactly the same way or make a brief detour (recommended) onto the tip of **Pointe du Guilligui** to see the superb dolmen.

Following narrow tracks and pleasant country lanes amid polders and partially drained salt marshes on the outward leg then returning via the dunes behind a wonderfully wild **Plage de Vougo**, this itinerary is particularly appealing on a blustery winter's day when a storm is brewing, the beach is empty, and fearful looking breakers are battering the string of rocks and islets along the shoreline. It's a walk I 'made up' from the map, only to get there and find somebody else had made it up before me, but the waymarking is not always unequivocal, consistent, or very permanent looking, so you will occasionally have to consult the book en route. For the hinterland stretch, the waymarks are yellow (to Wp.7), blue (Wps.7-9), and red (Wps.9-17).

| 2 | 3H | 12.75km | 75m / 75m | ↻ | 0 |
|---|---|---|---|---|---|

**Access:** by car or on foot from **Guisseny**.

### Strolls
The beach and dunes are readily accessible from the car parks on the coastal road.

To reach the start from the centre of **Guisseny**, take the 'Mairie'/'La Poste' road past the 'Bibliotheque', 'Maison Communale' and 'College' onto the **Port de Tresseny** shore. The itinerary starts at the car park 100 metres after the calvary, opposite 'Rue Eric Tabarly' in the 'Barrachou' neighbourhood.

**... a distinctive double outcrop of rock ...**

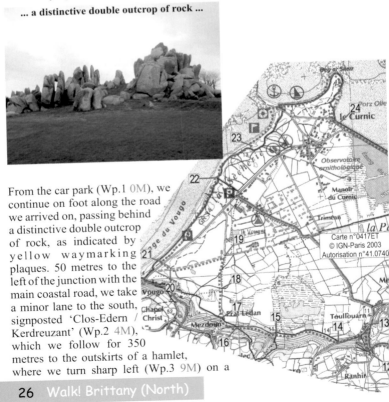

From the car park (Wp.1 0M), we continue on foot along the road we arrived on, passing behind a distinctive double outcrop of rock, as indicated by yellow waymarking plaques. 50 metres to the left of the junction with the main coastal road, we take a minor lane to the south, signposted 'Clos-Edern / Kerdreuzant' (Wp.2 4M), which we follow for 350 metres to the outskirts of a hamlet, where we turn sharp left (Wp.3 9M) on a grassy trail tunneling between tall hedgerows.

The trail soon feeds into a dirt track leading to another, narrower lane where we turn left (Wp.4 15M). Turning right on a dirt track 150 metres later (Wp.5), then forking left at the junction 275 metres after that (Wp.6 22M), we skirt the reclaimed farmland round **Poul Croaz** and follow a roughly surfaced track to a broad lane and multiple junction. Crossing the lane, we fork left (Wp.7 25M) on the **Kerlergon** farm access lane. When the lane swings sharp left toward the farm, we fork right (Wp.8 28M) on a narrow sunken track, maintaining a southerly direction towards the shallow hump of the uplands behind the flood plain. The track climbs gently, dwindling to a trail as it curves southwest to an inverted T-junction of lanes in the hamlet of **Kerhornaouen** (Wp.9 37M).

Heading due west then forking right at the Y-junction 150 metres later (Wp.10), we follow a minor lane as it traces an arc across the uplands overlooking the **Palud du Curnic** plain and **Plage de Vougou**. After carrying straight on at a crossroads (Wp.11 45M), we double back to the right at the next junction (Wp.12 49M) to descend from the low hills.

**Plage de Vougou**

Turning left at the next junction (Wp.13 52M), we dip down to pass a fountain, 75 metres after which, just before a bright blue gate, we leave the tarmac, forking right on a broad grassy track (Wp.14 56M).

The waymarked route detours up a small valley 500 metres later (Wp.15 63M), but it's as pleasant and practical to simply carry straight on, maintaining a westerly direction as the track climbs above the **Prat Lédan** polder before rejoining the waymarked route at a crossroads of tracks, where we turn right (Wp.16 67M).

We descend past a succession of private caravan berths, then fork right immediately after a cottage (Wp.17 70M) on a path leading to the network of tracks on the flood plain. We carry straight on at the junction with the first sandy track (Wp.18 74M) (the direct track to Wp.20 maybe cut by an electric fence) then turn left (leaving the waymarked itinerary) on the main, stabilized track (Wp.19 78M).

Shortly before the main track reaches the road, we turn right (Wp.20 83M) and cross the road to reach a broad trail behind the sand dunes (Wp.21 85M). We turn right here and simply follow the coast all the way back to the start, weaving back and forth between trail, dune and beach as the humour takes us. For the purposes of pacing progress, the trail passes a car park 100 metres later, then crosses a track accessing a second car park several hundred metres after that (Wp.22 95M). We then cross the campsite path and (Wp.23 102M) pass between the sailing club and small port to approach the **Beg ar Skeiz** headland.

After the headland, we can at low tide cut across the **Porz Oller** sandflats, but don't stray too far out as there's a permanent channel between the sea and the salt marsh, and a footbridge has to be crossed amid the dunes at the end of the **Le Curnic** dike. The main route is via a path along the back of the dike (Wp.24 123M), 50 metres after the end of which, we bear left (Wp.25 132M), and follow the narrow coastal path back past the **Dibennou** customs hut to our starting point.

# 5 GOULVEN: GOD'S GOLF COURSE

This is 'soft' walking in a sense, since the contours, colours, and paths are all easy on eye, heart, lungs, and legs, but it's none the less grand for that. First traversing a narrow band of reclaimed land, then meandering amid the **Dunes de Ker Emma**, we explore a landscape that put me in mind of nothing so much as a large and pleasingly wild golf course. The undulating terrain cloaked with tufty grass and patched with pits of sand, is what a really good golf course ought to be (I speak as someone with a strong allergy to ball games!), and to perfect the image it's riddled with rabbit burrows that are just the right dimension for a deity-sized golf ball, hence the conceit of God's Golf Course.

**Access:** on foot from **Goulven**.

From the car-park opposite the 'Berrou Regals de Bretagne' *patisserie* at the eastern entrance to **Goulven** (C3/D125 junction) (Wp.1 0M), we take the unnamed lane to the north, signposted 'Costa Draon'. Carrying straight on along a grassy track 150 metres later (signposted 'La Gare'), we turn left when we reach the D10 (Wp.2), then right 100 metres later (Wp.3 5M) and right again 50 metres after that (Wp.4), leaving the yellow waymarked route and following the GR along a well stabilised path beside the salt marshes of the ornithological reserve.

After crossing a car-park at the end of a dirt track, we fork left in front of a large shuttered farmhouse (Wp.5 13M) and stroll along a dike defending the polders behind the dunes, which get their name from the wife of the man who built the dike. 150 metres after a metal footbridge over a sluice gate, we turn right, sticking with the GR as it curves round the **Etang de Goulven** (Wp.6 23M). 250 metres later, we leave the main track beyond the *etang*, and fork left for the 'Maison des Dunes' (Wp.7 28M), an interpretation centre that we pass 400 metres later, after which a railway sleeper walkway takes us past a series of explanatory panels to a small information centre and cafeteria (Wp.8 40M).

Turning left, we follow a grassy trail alongside the **Maison des Dunes** car-park, beyond which, we fork right at a Y-junction (Wp.9 44M) to follow a sandy trail alongside a fence. Carrying straight on at a junction at the end of the fence (Wp.10 47M), we stay on the GR as it follows the main trail on the landward side of the dunes. After crossing another, unnamed car-park, (Wp.11 56M), we pass to the right of the isolated **St. Gouévroc** chapel. 50 metres after crossing the **Enez Vihan** car-park (Wp.12 67M), we bear right, away from the WW2 bunkers, to stay behind the dunes. We can either carry straight on along the grassy flats immediately behind the dunes, or keep bearing right to cross, 200 metres later, a footbridge over the trench of a tank trap (Wp.13 70M).

Thereafter, we simply follow the main sandy track to the east, re-crossing the anti-tank ditch then carrying straight on at a crossroads 300 metres later (Wp.14 80M), and again at the **Ar Méan** car-park (Wp.15 84M). At the northern end of the next car park (**Odé Vraz**, which can be inundated at high tide), we bear right on a path climbing onto the spit of dunes defining the **Anse de Kernic** (Wp.16 94M). Still favouring the southern side of the dunes, but actually in them now, we stroll along to their eastern tip overlooking the **Ar Ganol** channel (Wp.17 106M).

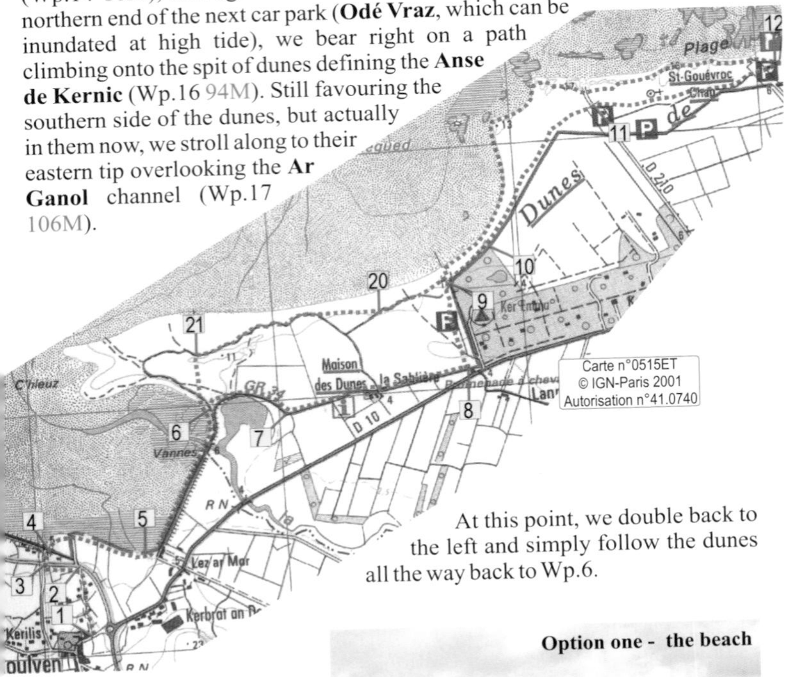

Carte n°0515ET
© IGN-Paris 2001
Autorisation n°41.0740

At this point, we double back to the left and simply follow the dunes all the way back to Wp.6.

**Option one - the beach**

There are three ways this can be done. One, at low tide stroll along the packed sands below the high water mark. Two, retrace your steps to Wp.16 then follow the flat grassy trails just behind the dunes. Three, actually walk through the dunes on their seaward side.

The last option is possibly the most arduous, especially since to begin with there is no single path, only a series of ways winding through the spiky sea grass, but it's by far the most interesting walking. That said, please do respect the signs and fencing put in place to prevent erosion.

There's really no call for description here, but for the purposes of pacing progress, we re-cross the track behind the **Odé Vraz** car park 30 metres north of Wp.16 (120M), then cross the trail behind the **Ar Méan** car-park (Wp.18

130M), and the continuation of the cross track at Wp.14 (Wp.19 134M). At the **Enez Vihan** car-park (Wp.12 145M), our outward and return routes momentarily intersect before we immediately bear right to continue along the line of the dunes, passing the outcrops of rock behind the chapel.

Carte n°0515ET
© IGN-Paris 2001
Autorisation n°41.0740

The two routes come within a hair's breadth of touching at Wp.11 (155M), but again we bear right to stay in the dunes, weaving round rocks and through tufty clumps of grass to pass a toppled pillbox/machine-gun post, favouring the seaward side when in doubt.

Eventually, we return to Wp.9 (173M), where we again bear right to traverse the close cropped sward directly behind the dunes, essentially off path but following a fairly obvious route marked by intermittent stumpy wayposts. When the main wayposted route diverges from the dunes along the line a of shallow ditch (Wp.20 178M), we carry straight on, shadowing the dunes then climbing into their midst again, in line with the radio mast beyond the **Grève de Goulven**. There's an un-mappable maze of paths, half paths and trodden ways webbing the western end of the dunes, but as long as you stay on the main trail in the middle of the dunes, and keep on heading WSW you can't go far wrong, and in any case will soon come across more wayposts. At a crossroads some 500 metres after we returned to the dunes (immediately after another waypost and several hundred metres short of the end of the dunes) (Wp.21 187M), we turn left to rejoin our outward route at Wp.6.

# 6 MOGUÉRIEC: GOLDEN SANDS & GREEN LANES

So long as you time the low water crossing right, this gentle loop round the **River Guillec** is not likely to set your pulse racing, since compared with most of the west coast, the land behind the fishing port of **Moguériec** is not a natural stage for the bluster and drama of the elements. Nonetheless, the sandy estuary, lovely dunes, healthy woods and a fine riverside path conspire to make this an itinerary of attractive contrasts, and the barefoot crossing of the bay should appeal to adventurous children. The estuary at the start of the walk can be traversed with relative ease for about an hour on either side of low tide. You'll see instantly if you turn up on spec whether it's feasible or not, but best to plan ahead. Tide tables are available from newsagents, Tourist Information Offices or on http://tide.frbateaux.net. We do get our feet wet (boots off at Wp.2), but by the time we've trudged through dry sand beyond the watercourse, a towel is not essential.

| | | | | | | |
|---|---|---|---|---|---|---|
| 2 | 2¾ H | 11.3 km | /\/\ | 100m ↗ 100m ↘ | | 3 |

**Access:** on foot from **Moguériec**.

**Strolls**
The **Circuit de la Vallée du Guillec** from the **St. Jacques** car-park on the D10 (Wp.10).

Setting off from the **Port de Moguériec** car-park in front the 'Marin' bar/hotel/restaurant (Wp.1 0M), we stroll onto the docks where a sign indicates that this is the start of one of the **Santiago de Compostella** routes.

**Crossing the estuary**

Taking the second staircase on the right of the quay, we pick our way across the weedy puddles in the harbour (SE) to the narrowest, shallowest stretch of the watercourse (Wp.2 5M). After fording the river, we head due east across the sandbank to a tiny beach just south of the jumble of rocks off to our left, where we join the GR34 (Wp.3 14M).

Feet de-sanded and re-shod (not counted in subsequent timings), we turn right and follow the sandy path winding through the dunes, forking right at two major Y-junctions to stay beside the river (Wp.4 19M & Wp.5 26M). The GR soon crosses a small car-park (Wp.6 29M) and the end of a tarmac lane, beyond which the ground becomes firmer. Turning right at a signposted junction (Wp.7 36M), we approach a lovely old mill, shortly before which the trail veers away from the water's edge to join a lane, on which we again turn right (Wp.8 46M).

When the GR turns right at an attractive stone bridge (Wp.9 52M), we carry straight on and cross the D10 (some care required as it's a fast stretch of road) into the St. Jacques car-park, where there's a sign for the 'Circuit de la Vallée

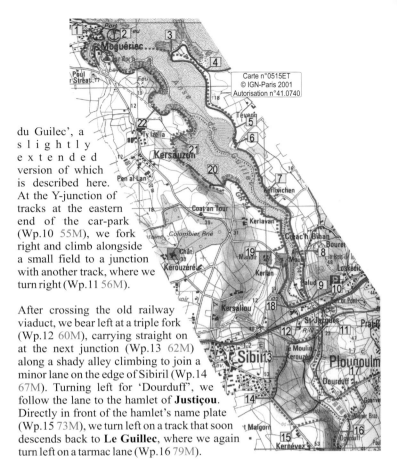

du Guilec', a slightly extended version of which is described here. At the Y-junction of tracks at the eastern end of the car-park (Wp.10 55M), we fork right and climb alongside a small field to a junction with another track, where we turn right (Wp.11 56M).

After crossing the old railway viaduct, we bear left at a triple fork (Wp.12 60M), carrying straight on at the next junction (Wp.13 62M) along a shady alley climbing to join a minor lane on the edge of Sibiril (Wp.14 67M). Turning left for 'Dourduff', we follow the lane to the hamlet of **Justiçou**. Directly in front of the hamlet's name plate (Wp.15 73M), we turn left on a track that soon descends back to **Le Guillec**, where we again turn left on a tarmac lane (Wp.16 79M).

The lane passes behind a fish farm and climbs towards **Plougoulm**, where we turn left at a T-junction (Wp.17 84M) to return to the river. Staying on the right bank of the river, we follow a dirt track back under the viaduct to the **St. Jacques** car-park where we re-cross the D10 to rejoin the GR at Wp.9 (99M)

Crossing the stone bridge, we follow the lane through the hamlet of **St. Jacques**, on the far side of which we recover the coast path at a waymarked turning on our right (Wp.18 102M). The remainder of the walk follows the GR all the way back to **Moguériéc** and is clearly waymarked/signposted throughout. The path climbs to the **Manoir de Kerlan**, where we rejoin the St. Jacques' lane for 100 metres before turning right on a track skirting fields (Wp.19 110M). After crossing a tiny lane (Wp.20 122M), we climb away from the river to avoid private property before descending through woodland back to the water's edge. After emerging from the woodland, we cross a first dirt track (Wp.21 132M) and briefly intersect with a second (Wp.22 140M) before arriving back at the fishing port. Contouring round the inlet of the port, a final field side path brings us back to the start.

A markedly varied itinerary, this walk explores the coast and countryside around **Santec,** the village that gave birth to the 'Johnnies', the onion sellers who cycled round Britain selling their produce and cementing the image of the stereotypical Frenchman (beret, stripy T-shirt and so forth) in the British psyche. After crossing the sandy fields that are still heavily farmed today (notably for carrots and onions), we meander through dense woodland, skirt a marshy estuary, traverse extensive dunes, then take to the beach for a long loop round the coast. The GR is not terribly interesting here (and there are stretches that IGN have mis-mapped), which is why we've elected to make this a 'low-water' walks using the beach. Some of these low-water walks require close consultation of the tide tables (see http://tide.frbateaux.net or pick up a copy from any newsagents or tobacconist), but in this instance the way will only be cut by the highest tides. All the 'underwater' bits of this itinerary should be practical throughout the day save for an hour or so either side of high tide. The right of way used after Wp.3 is customary rather than statutory, but the day we did the walk an entire family (grandfather down to grandchildren) were out on their knees selecting potatoes and confirmed that this was 'a path'. As it happens, it's not really a path, just a way along the edge of the field, but there shouldn't be a problem so long as nobody goes blundering across any crops.

* The **Embruns** snack bar is a good basic eatery at the end of the walk, including proper chips from local potatoes. Otherwise there are three slightly more sophisticated looking establishments at **Drossen** (Wp.19).

**Access:** by car

| **Strolls** |
| --- |
| (a) the **Forêt Domaniale** (see Wp.13 & 18 for access) offers easy walking on a variety of trails and tracks. |
| (b) at low tide, **Ile de Siec** from Wp.19. |

The walks starts from the 'Cale de Pouldu' car-park beside 'Les Embruns' snack bar in the coastal hamlet of **Pouldu**, signposted from the centre of **Santec**. Setting off from the car-park (Wp.1 0M), we stroll along the **Roscoff** road in front of the **Embruns** restaurant and take the branch road forking off to the left for 'Terrain de Foot'/'Aire du Palud'. 300 metres along this road, just before a turning on the left for 'Menuiserie'/'Aire de picnic', we turn right (Wp.2 6M) on a grassy track traversing sandy fields. After crossing the **Roscoff** road 150 metres later, we continue on a narrow tarmac lane past house N°245.

A little over 100 metres later, the lane swings sharp left and becomes a dirt track (Wp.3 11M). We leave the lane here, before the end of the tarmac, maintaining a southwesterly direction along the right hand side of the hedge, ten metres along which we find an arched gateway leading into a small field. Staying on the left hand side of the field alongside the wall, we soon join a farm track, which is surfaced as it passes between houses to a junction with a lane (Wp.4 14M).

Turning left, we follow this lane for 350 metres, then turn right in front of

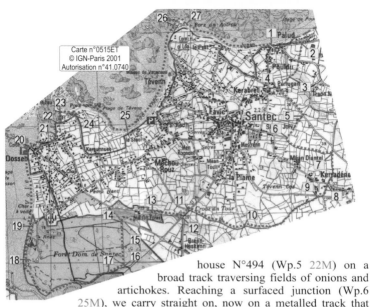

house N°494 (Wp.5 22M) on a broad track traversing fields of onions and artichokes. Reaching a surfaced junction (Wp.6 25M), we carry straight on, now on a metalled track that curves east. At a T-junction with a narrow lane (Wp.7 33M), we turn right and cross a broader road 300 metres later (Wp.8 38M). Continuing to the south, still on tarmac, we follow the lane as it swings round to the 'Riou'/'Prince de Bretagne' vegetable packing plant, where we fork left (Wp.9 40M) on a very narrow lane traversing rolling agricultural plain. We stick with this lane, ignoring all branches (including a major turning on the right Wp.10 51M), until it crosses the D75, at which point we turn left (Wp.11 60M), then right 75 metres later (Wp.12) to enter the **Forêt Domaniale**.

The sudden plunge into a deep green tunnel comes as a striking contrast to the wide open sandy fields traversed so far, but look a little closer and you'll see that even the forest has to root itself in soil that is largely sand. At a Y-junction 300 metres from the road (Wp.13 66M), we fork left to follow a narrow path meandering along the perimeter of the woods.

**Alongside the estuary**

After crossing a minor road (Wp.14 74M), we take the middle of three tracks (signposted N°3) into the main part of the *forêt*, carrying straight on (S) at a crossroads 50 metres later and again at two successive junctions (Wps. 15 78M & 16 81M), after which the path bears right to join a sandy track beside a marshy estuary (Wp.17 84M).

We follow the track round to the mouth of the estuary, where we can either continue on the sand-flats or (recommended) take the picket-fenced path traversing the 'Dune Domaniale de Santec'.

The dune path passes a beautifully located campsite (Wp.18 101M) before reaching a T-junction with a sandy track (Wp.19 109M), at which point I recommend taking to the beach to avoid the asphalt and housing at the southern end of the hamlet of **Dossen**.

**Dossen** *colonie de vacance*

After nearly a kilometre on the beach, we bear east, directly behind the **Ile de Siec**, to regain solid ground beside the **Dossen** coastguard porta-kabins, where the day's tides are posted, including the hour at which the island is encircled with water (Wp.20 122M).

We now briefly follow the GR on the lane heading inland from the far end of the dockside car-park. After going through a pedestrian alley (Wp.21 126M), we turn left to reach the end of a second lane, where a stretch of the coastal path proper (Wp.22) leads us onto the **Beg ar Billou** peninsula. Forking right (Wp.23 130M), we follow a sandy track, inland once again, to a junction in front of a house called 'Penn ar Bed' (Wp.24 134M).

Turning sharp left, we leave the GR and take to the beach again, crossing the **Porz ar Vil** harbour and picking our way through the rocks to reach the long **Plage de Tévenn**, where there's a pedestrian signpost indicating the way to 'Ilot Roc-Kroum' (Wp.25 146M). At the far end of **Plage de Tévenn**, we once again briefly intersect with the GR, either via the last hard accessing the beach or scrambling directly over the boulders of the sea defences to cross the **Corn al Loa** headland (Wp.26 162M) before rejoining the beach (Wp.27 165M). The starting point is reached via the second access lane in **Cale de Pouldu**, from where a narrow path alongside a seafront field leads directly into the car-park.

# 8 CARANTEC: ÎLE CALLOT - SUBMARINE STROLL

Splashing about in rock pools and poking about to see what's lurking under individual rocks is pretty much an essential pastime on the Breton coast and in this walk, the first of two extreme low-water walks, we celebrate this tradition by walking 'underwater', taking advantage of the tides and a couple of causeways to explore the tiny **Île Callot** beside the holiday resort of **Carantec**.

The channel between the mainland and the island can be crossed about three hours before low tide, though you may have to wait a little longer during bigger tides. It's best to start as early as possible, not because there's much risk of getting stranded, but for the pleasure of reaching this popular island before anyone else. Tide tables are available at Tourist Information Centres, newsagents and on http://tide.frbateaux.net, and are posted at the start of the walk.

**Access:** on foot from **Carantec**.

From **Carantec** port (Wp.1 0M), we head north along the '*Chaussée submersible*', which may still be underwater if (as recommended) you're setting off well before low tide. 150 metres along the surfaced road, when it swings right through an S-bend, we fork left (Wp.2) on a natural embankment curving toward a red navigation beacon.

This route is the one first uncovered by the falling tide and you may see locals using it in their cars - not recommended unless you know what you're doing, where you're going, and exactly how you're getting there! There is, however, no problem negotiating it on foot. Passing to the right of the first little islet and to the left of the second, we reach an old shingle causeway (Wp.3 13M).

We cross the causeway and bear left to circle the **Ar Run** headland, still 'underwater'. Passing between the headland and the **L'Hôpital** islet, we reach the first of the main island's beaches, **Plage de Park an Aod** (Wp.4 18M), at the far end of which, we turn right on a hard then left on the island's solitary lane (Wp.5 28M), passing **Callot**'s principal public infrastructure: a diminutive school, a phone booth, and the public lavatories!

The chapel after Wp.6

At a well at the foot of the small rise topped by the chapel, we fork right (Wp.6 37M) to visit the chapel, beyond which we rejoin the continuation of the lane, now a dirt track (Wp.7 40M).

The track soon dwindles to a trail, which we follow to the **Penn ar Waremm** nature reserve at the head of the island, where there's a cross and a small orientation table (Wp.8 49M).

There are various mini-loops round the headland and it should be possible to return via the beaches on the western flank of the island, but since that side shelves more steeply toward the main navigation channel and will probably still be submerged at this stage, I recommend looping round the headland then descending onto the northernmost beach on the eastern side, behind the large white painted rock of the **Tourelle Mazarin**.

Back 'underwater', we pick our way across the rocks (watch out for slippery patches of seaweed) then stroll along the flats amid the scattered rocks facing **Saint-Pol-de-Leon**, following the tracks left by tractors harvesting the local oyster beds. An easy stroll brings us back to **Plage de Park an Aod** and Wp.5 (78M), where we bear right to follow the lane and the paths alongside it to the main, surfaced causeway (Wp.9 88M), which we take back to the start.

Carte n°0615ET
© IGN-Paris 1996
Autorisation n°41.0740

# 9 LE DIBEN TO TERENEZ: THE TOAD, THE PRIEST'S SEAT & NAPOLEON'S HAT

I do a variant of this walk nearly every day, yet never tire of it as there's always something new to see in the subtle shifts of the falling light, the quicksilver mutations of the sea, the seasonal variations in the wildfowl, and more dramatic if less common sightings of seals, dolphins and a colony of mink that escaped from a flooded farm. If that isn't recommendation enough, suffice to say that though this area is not particularly famous, whenever a book or article wants to illustrate the coastal path, it will almost invariably feature a photo taken somewhere along this itinerary. Setting off from the small fishing port of **Le Diben**, we trace a complicated route through the hinterland overlooking the **Baie de Morlaix** then return from the tiny haven of **Térénez** via the coastal path, visiting in turn the landmark rocks of the title: *Le Crapaud*, *La Chaise du Curé*, and *Le Chapeau du Napoléon*. In warm weather, a towel and swimming costume are essential.

*in **Térénez**

**Access:** by car or bus from **Morlaix**.

### Strolls/Short Versions
There are three obvious short versions between **Le Diben** and **Le Guerzit** (turning right at Wp.14), between **Le Guerzit** and **St. Samson** (turning right at Wp.17 or 18), and between **Térénez** and **St. Samson** (turning right at Wp.25). The headlands on either side of **Le Diben** are excellent places for a stroll during a storm, though do take care - the waves are a lot bigger than you.

The walk starts from the main car-park at **Le Diben** port, which is accessible by 'Rue du Port' just below the 'Café-Alimentacion Masson' on the D46. To begin with, we follow the GR waymarks back into **Le Diben**. Fifty metres above the car-park (Wp.1 0M), we take 'Rue de Pors Louarn', forking left after 150 metres into the driveway of house N°5 (Wp.2), which leads to a shoreside path. The path debouches on another road (Wp.3 5M), at which point we turn left then right, up towards the 'Café du Port', where we fork left on the 'Venelle de Perros' (Wp.4). When this alley joins the 'Impasse du Quinquai' 100 metres later (Wp.5), we leave the GR and bear right, back towards the D46.

Crossing the road, we take 'Allée des Mimosas' (Wp.6 10M), which almost immediately dwindles to a footpath, at the end of which, we bear left on a narrow lane (Wp.7 12M). Turning left again at the 'Impasse de Kerverot' (Wp.8 15M 9.14), we descend to join a grassy, faintly obscure path climbing past a *lavoir* and spring. Turning right for 'Kerhamon' at a T-junction (Wp.9 18M), we rejoin the network of lanes behind **Le Diben** (Wp.10 19M). We turn left then right on 'Rue du Poul Du' (Wp.11 21M), which brings us to a junction with 'Rue de Bourhiol Vras' (Wp.12 27M) where we bear left to reach the D46 again. 25 metres to the right is a signposted path (Wp.13 28M) descending to the coast (beware if the steps are damp - they'll have your feet out from under you quicker than a conjuror's tablecloth).

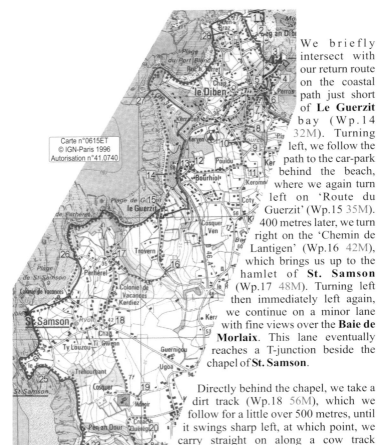

We briefly intersect with our return route on the coastal path just short of **Le Guerzit** bay (Wp.14 32M). Turning left, we follow the path to the car-park behind the beach, where we again turn left on 'Route du Guerzit' (Wp.15 35M). 400 metres later, we turn right on the 'Chemin de Lantigen' (Wp.16 42M), which brings us up to the hamlet of **St. Samson** (Wp.17 48M). Turning left then immediately left again, we continue on a minor lane with fine views over the **Baie de Morlaix**. This lane eventually reaches a T-junction beside the chapel of **St. Samson**.

Directly behind the chapel, we take a dirt track (Wp.18 56M), which we follow for a little over 500 metres, until it swings sharp left, at which point, we carry straight on along a cow track (Wp.19 64M). This is very much a working cow track and is in daily use. If it's impassably 'muddy', stay on the main track to rejoin the road through Kermebel, turn right then first right again to rejoin the described itinerary at Wp.20. The cow track joins a tiny lane 75 metres later (Wp.20), on which we turn right. The lane soon bears left and descends toward a restored millhouse. When the lane curves left into the millhouse garden, we fork right (Wp.21 71M) on a path climbing to a junction of country lanes.

We cross onto the 'Chemin Pen ar C'har' (Wp.22 74M), which we follow down to the right, where it becomes a tiny path descending back to the road. After descending toward **Térénez** for fifty metres, we fork right on the amusingly named 'Rue de Paris' (it wasn't actually the road to Paris, but was jokingly called that by a couple of holidaying artists, then the *mairie* formalized the jest) (Wp.23 76M) which descends past new houses and a mind-bogglingly miniature fisherman's cottage to rejoin the coastal path (Wp.24 78M). For refreshments, turn left, for the remainder of the walk, turn right.

After all the twists and turns of the outward leg, the return is a doddle, as we simply follow the coastal path all the way back to **Le Diben**, so it's books in

Plage de St. Samson

the bag and eyes on the horizon. For the purposes of pacing progress, we pass the tiny beach of **Ty Louzou** (Wp.25 91M) then curve round the headland to the double rock of **Le Crapaud**, unmistakable when you're alongside it, though looking rather more like a mole on the approach.

La Chaise du Curé

At low tide, we can descend onto the long beach of **St. Samson** 75 metres after **Le Crapaud**, otherwise, we stick with the waymarked path as it passes behind the former **Colonie de Vacances**. Either way, at the far end of the **Plage de St. Samson**, we recover the coastal path proper (Wp.26 113M), soon passing another distinctive and readily identifiable rock formation, traditionally known as **La Chaise du Curé**, though some now refer to it as **La Pile des Assiettes**. We then intersect with our outward route behind **Le Guerzit** (again, beach walking an option at low tide) (129M).

At Wp.14, we continue straight on, soon passing the somewhat less distinctive rock of **Le Chapeau de Napoleon**. At the foot of the steep **Analouestan** headland, we ignore a first stepped ascent to the right (Wp.27 142M) and carry straight on to climb directly onto the heights, from where we have superb views along the coast and out to sea. We then descend back to the water's edge and follow the coastal path as it curves round the bay of **Port Blanc**, beyond which a clear path crosses a driveway (Wp.28 160M) on the final headland separating us from **Le Diben** and our starting point.

## STOP PRESS

Walk 9 Following the exceptional storms of March 2008, the coastal path around Plougasnou has been closed while the local authorities 'assess the situation'. Local walkers have already assessed the situation, cut the ribbon, and carried on walking as usual. However, at the time of going to press the path is still officially closed. The only points at which you are liable to encounter (very minor) inconvenience are north of Wp.25 and southwest of Wp.15 where the sea has piled stones over the path, making walking a little hard underfoot. The path on all other itineraries affected by the storm has already been repaired or will be repaired by the Summer of 2008.

# 10 PLOUGASNOU: VALLÉE DES MOULINS & BEG AN FRY

One of the finest stretches of coast in Brittany and one of the most arduous, the wild terrain between **Plougasnou** and **Poul Rodou** should be a must-do on any visiting rambler's list. Combined with the lovely **Vallée des Moulins** it makes for a superb if gruelling circuit. The **Vallée des Moulins** can be muddy in winter, but otherwise there are no major obstacles en route except, of course, for the endless ups and downs of the coastal path, which ought not to be tackled if you're not accustomed to strenuous walking. There are so many of these ups and downs, some small, several huge, all steep, that an accurate assessment of the accumulated climb would call for a team of surveyors. My estimate is based on an on-the-hoof reckoning and doesn't sound terribly tough, but the best indication I can give is that, no matter how used to climbing mountains you may be, your legs will feel the strain of this walk. There's something about going up then down, up then down for ever and a day that is far more wearing than simply doing a straight 1000 metre ascent.

5 | 4½ H | 22.5km | 400m / 400m | ⟳ | 4

## Short Versions
(a) **Sentier de la Vallée des Moulins** (see Wps.6 to 22)
(b) If you can come as a two car party, the comparatively short coastal walk between Wps.32 and 37 or 40 is more than rigorous enough to make a satisfying outing of itself.

**Stroll**
Vallée des Moulins (see Wps.7 & 12)

**Access:** on foot from **Plougasnou** or **St. Jean du Doigt**.

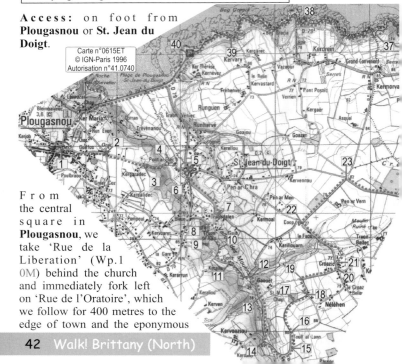

Carte n°0615ET
© IGN-Paris 1996
Autorisation n°41.0740

From the central square in **Plougasnou**, we take 'Rue de la Liberation' (Wp.1 0M) behind the church and immediately fork left on 'Rue de l'Oratoire', which we follow for 400 metres to the edge of town and the eponymous oratory (Wp.2 5M). We then carry straight on along 'Route de Kergaradec', until it swings sharp right and we maintain direction (E) (Wp.3 10M) on a waymarked path descending past a *lavoir*.

At the crossroads at the bottom the hill, we turn right (Wp.4 14M) on a track that feeds into a lane before joining the main road through **St. Jean du Doigt**, where we again turn right (Wp.5 17M). We then fork left from the central square on a lane signposted 'Vallée des Moulins' (Wp.6 19M). 300 metres later, the waymarked trail doubles back to the left on a dirt track (Wp.7 25M), but we stay on the lane as it passes a ramshackle wooden barn and climbs on the far side of the valley to the hamlet of 'Kericuff', where we turn left on the 'Sentier de la Vallée des Moulins' (Wp.8 28M).

The tarmac peters out beside a house 75 metres later and we fork left at a Y-junction (Wp.9) to follow a broad grassy track that dwindles to a path as it skirts a private caravan site. Turning right on the site's access track (Wp.10 32M), then left 50 metres later, we descend to an apparent dead end at the gates of the **Goris** millhouse, where a path climbs to the right, circumnavigating the mill (Wp.11 35M).

Our trail then dips into the valley below a large mill pond and crosses onto the eastern flank of the valley, where we come to a T-junction with a dirt track (Wp.12 39M). For the stroll, follow the waymarked route climbing to the left before descending back to Wp.7. For the full itinerary, we turn right, staying in the valley, which at this stage is a great green lung of shrubbery and raggledy-taggledy oak. The track climbs to a junction (Wp.13 43M) where we continue up the peaceful valley, undisturbed by any sound apart from the trickling of water, the warblings of wood pigeons, and the breeze rustling the leaves in the trees. When the track comes to a T-junction with a road, we turn left and climb toward the farm hamlet of **Le Cran** (Wp.14 49M).

Ignoring a waymarked track off to the right (Wp.15

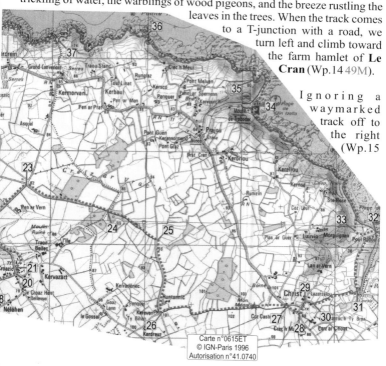

54M), we stay on the road as it passes the house of 'Toul al Lan' then fork left at the next bend on a dirt track signposted 'Sentier de la Vallée des Moulins' (Wp.16 57M). The track curves between heavily cultivated fields, passing the bucolic **Chapelle de St. Mélàr** (Wp.17 61M) before entering another farm hamlet, 'Corn ar Mejou' (Wp.18 63M), which is where we begin the least attractive part of the itinerary, traversing the agricultural plateau behind the coast.

Turning left, we continue on dirt track and the 'Sentier de la Vallée des Moulins'. At the next T-junction, we turn right on a surfaced track (Wp.19 65M), then left when the track joins a lane (Wp.20 69M). 50 metres later, waymarks indicate a brief detour from the road (Wp.21), which we rejoin for another 300 metres until it comes to a large 'Coop Agri Bretagne' barn (Wp.22 77M). For Short Version A, carry straight on and follow the waymarked routes back to Wps.7 or 12. For the full walk, we leave the 'Sentier de la Vallée des Moulins' and turn right for 'Pen ar Vern', still on tarmac.

At the multiple junction after the **Pen ar Vern** farm, we turn right on an unmarked dirt track (Wp.23 84M), heading toward a couple of scruffy coppices. The track eventually comes to a Y-junction where we fork right (away from the 'Circuit de Beg an Fry' directional arrow) (Wp.24 95M). When this branch track, which is surfaced for the last 150 metres, reaches a T-junction with a lane, we turn right (Wp.25 102M). 600 metres later, the lane passes through the scattered farming hamlet of **Runtannic**, where a road leads in from the right, opposite which we turn left on a dirt track (Wp.26 110M). This track, the most agreeable of those followed on the plateau, meanders amid banks of bracken and relatively small fields before passing a lovingly tended megalithic burial chamber, the **Gwele Sant Yann**, 300 metres after which we reach the main road through **Christ** (Wp.27 128M).

Following the waymarked route, we turn right, then left at the calvary just before the endearingly named **Bar Ouf** (Wp.28). 100 metres later, we turn right (Wp.29) then fork left 50 metres after that (Wp.30), leaving the asphalt to follow a shady trail that gradually broadens to a track, which is surfaced as it approaches the main lane down to **Poul Rodou**.

50 metres before the lane (Wp.31 139M), we turn left on a dirt track that meanders along the high ground before dwindling to a trail dropping down to feed into another track that joins the GR 250 metres later (Wp.32 148M), just next to the celebrated **Kaplan** café-bookshop.

... remorseless rollercoaster ...

We now simply turn left and follow the GR all the way back to **Plougasnou**, a stretch of path that is so consistently lovely, reading about it would be a criminal waste of time.

The bullet points that follow serve merely for pacing progress and, in the later stages, indicating ways to escape the remorseless roller-coaster of the *sentier cotier* if lungs and legs can take no more.

- When the track reaches a signposted T-junction, we turn right (Wp.33 152M)

- The **Beg an Fry** path climbs away from the **Moulin de Troboder** picnic area (Wp.34 183M)

- After the steep climb up **Beg an Fry**, we turn right at a wayposted junction to descend (!) back toward the coast (Wp.35 198M)

**West of Runglaz**

- We pass the **Pointe Runglaz**, distinguishable from the other headlands in that it's a rockier promontory with browner vegetation. A good spot for a picnic. (Wp.36 227M)

- After two very steep climbs, the first broken by railway sleeper steps, we reach our first 'escape route', a broad trail climbing from a tall concrete chimney to a track that leads to the coastal road, which is considerably less strenuous and considerably less enjoyable (Wp.37 250M).

- Escape route two (Wp.38 274M)

- Escape route three (narrow and frequently overgrown) (Wp.39 292M).

- The coastal path enters a large parking bay (Wp.40 307M) beside the road, which we follow back to **Plougasnou**.

# 11 CRANOU: THE ETERNAL FOREST

Every Breton forest boasts it's own legend and **Cranou**, which used to furnish the timbers for the shipyards in **Brest**, is no exception. The story goes that Saint Conval wanted to build an oratory in the **Bois du Gars** between **Hanvec** and **L'Hôpital-Camfrout**, but the dendrophiliac lord of the manor wasn't having any airy-fairy priest chopping his trees down and chased the importunate cleric away. The owner of **Cranou** proved a more congenial patron and told Conval to take all the wood he wanted, whereupon the saint cursed the **Bois du Gars**, declaring it would be so badly deforested there wouldn't be enough timber to fashion a tiller, while **Cranou** would be blessed with abundant trees for all eternity. Seems to have worked, too. At **Gars** there's nothing but thickets and coppicing, but **Cranou** is still a forest worthy of the name. True, there's been extensive replantation with pine, but there are still some magnificent oak, beech and birch, and a fair few yew, too, and some patches of the forest are so deep and dark they'd do very nicely for a fairytale. There's no refreshment en route, but the **Hanvec Restaurant du Gare** (see access details) does a decent litre-of-plonk-on-the-table *menu du jour* that's popular with local labourers and passing lorry drivers. N.B. If you don't fancy ducking under the fences at Wp.9, fork right at Wp.6, rejoining the described itinerary at Wp.14.

**Access:** by car

Most people will probably arrive via the D18 between **Le Faou** and **Sizun**. If coming from the north, take the minor road on the left (signposted 'Maisons Breton'/'Pennarun') between the **Hanvec** 'Restaurant du Gare' (the station's actually at the outlying hamlet of **Roudouhir**) and the level crossing, then turn left at the crossroads beside the calvary.

*Carte n°0517ET*
*© IGN-Paris 2003*
*Autorisation n°41.0740*

The walk starts 100 metres south of the junction with the D42 on a track branching off the 'Nellach' turning. If you're arriving from the south, fork right at the 'Croix de Boudouguen' between **Hanvec** and the train station, carrying straight on at the next calvary to reach the D42. There's room to park at the junction of the track and the lane leading to **Nellach**.

We set off along the main forestry track (Wp.1 0M), then turn left at the barrier restricting vehicular access to the forest (Wp.2 2M) and climb along a broad trail that doubles as a watershed during wet weather. Carrying straight on at junctions with a track from **Nellach** (Wp.3 8M) and a path descending to the right (Wp.4 16M), we stroll across more level land along a tree lined alley flanked by fields.

When the alley reaches a T-junction with another track (Wp.5 22M), we turn right, continuing along the fringes of the forest, occasionally diverging from the main trail, which maybe intermittently waterlogged. Ignoring a couple of forestry tracks descending to the right (Wp.6 41M), we eventually reach the lane accessing the hamlet of **Le Labou**.

At this point, we leave the waymarked route (white dots) that we've been following so far and carry straight on, maintaining an easterly direction on a broad dirt track (Wp.7 45M). The eastbound track passes a branch off to the left (Wp.8 52M), 400 metres after which, it ends at a couple of electric fences (Wp.9 57M). The next 250 metres are on private land and are not a right -of-way, but it's a route commonly used by local hunters and ramblers, and is marked as a path on the IGN maps.

Ducking under or stepping over the single strand fences, we follow a narrow trodden way along the edge of a field, in the far corner of which, we cross another single strand fence to join the **GR37** just short of the D42 (Wp.10 61M).

We now follow the GR through the heart of the forest. Turning right and ignoring two forks off to the left (Wps.11 & 12), we cross a firebreak framing an interred gas pipe on the edge of the forest (Wp.13 72M). Ignoring a turning on the right 100 metres later (Wp.14), we stay on the GR as it descends along the main track toward a rushing stream. We then turn right at a waymarked junction (Wp.15 84M) on a narrower trail. This, too, may be waterlogged in its earlier, level stages, in which case a trodden way winds alongside the main trail amid the mossy humps of the forest floor.

The trail then climbs between young oak and beech to a junction with a logging track (Wp.16 92M) where we bear left then turn left 50 metres later on an obscure but well waymarked path descending through the dark heart of the wood (Wp.17).

**Evading the puddles**

When the path joins one of the arterial forestry tracks (Wp.18 99M), we turn right to reach a multiple crossroads at the 'Maison Forestière La Roche Noire' (Wp.19 106M). Forking left (not the bridleway 90° turn), we continue along the GR as it traverses an alley of towering oak and birch before descending to a junction with another major track, the **Ligne de la Carriole** (Wp.20 120M).

We carry straight on then leave the GR 50 metres later, turning right on a delightful trail climbing back into the woods (Wp.21). After forking left at a Y-junction (Wp.22 123M), we climb to another broad track beside the D42 (Wp.23 131M).

Crossing the track, we follow a very faint way (virtually off path) winding through the woods parallel to the road for 125 metres to reach the start of another track beside a couple of picnic tables (Wp.24). Bearing right, we follow this track up to rejoin the main track just short of Wp.2.

# 12 DRENNEC: LAC DU DRENNEC & CIRCUIT DU MOUGAU

Though it doesn't visit any of the iconic summits or famous marshes of the **Monts d'Arrée**, this is one of the area's most satisfying walks because it's so very varied, beginning with a stroll beside a most domestic lake, then visiting a particularly fine megalithic monument, traversing a small bog, climbing onto wild windy upland and following a picturesque stream back to the lake before returning to the start via an attractive little wood. The tour of the lake is obvious and the **Circuit du Mougau** is sign or wayposted at all key junctions (except the junction just before Wp.12), so once you've read through the description and got to the start, the book can be safely stashed.

| | | | | | | |
|---|---|---|---|---|---|---|
| 4 | 3½ H | 16.25km | | 250m / 250m | ↻ | 1 |

**Access:** by car

| **Stroll** | **Short Versions** |
|---|---|
| **Circuit des Korrigans** from **Mougau Bihan**. | Strolling along the lake shore between Wps.7 & 30 breaks the itinerary into two obvious circuits. |

The walks stars from the hamlet of **Le Drennec**, accessible from the D764 midway between **Commana** and **Sizun**. One kilometre west of the 'Ecomusée des Moulins de Kerouet', turn south for 'Gouzorvern' and continue heading south through 'Kerféos' for the 'Barrage de Drennec'. Park beside the recreation/picnic area just before the dam.

From the car-park (Wp.1 0M), we cross the recreation/picnic area and follow the well tailored, pushchair-friendly path round the northern shore of the lake.

There's nowhere to go wrong here, indeed it's all so straightforward we might be strolling round the pond in a municipal park if it wasn't for the size of the lake, so just enjoy the easy walking, crossing another picnic area at the end of a dirt track after 1km (Wp.2 13M) then a carpark 900 metres later (Wp.3 23M).

**The lake, partially drained**

The lake is shielded by a band of woodland as the path heads north to the hamlet of **Kerret**, where we bear right (Wp.4 27M) to reach a minor road crossing a dike (Wp.5 35M). Turning right then right again 100 metres later (Wp.6), we continue along the lake-shore path until we reach the tennis court, carpark and access road behind the **Centre Nautique de l'Arrée** (Wp.7 46M).

This is where we leave the lake and join the 'Circuit du Mougau'. Turning left behind the *centre nautique*, we follow the road northeast then east to a junction, where a slip path (Wp.8 51M) cuts through to the **Kermabil** farm

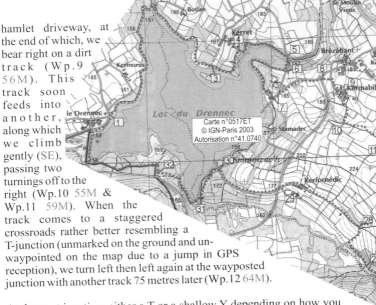

hamlet driveway, at the end of which, we bear right on a dirt track (Wp.9 56M). This track soon feeds into another, along which we climb gently (SE), passing two turnings off to the right (Wp.10 55M & Wp.11 59M). When the track comes to a staggered crossroads rather better resembling a T-junction (unmarked on the ground and un-waypointed on the map due to a jump in GPS reception), we turn left then left again at the wayposted junction with another track 75 metres later (Wp.12 64M).

At the next junction, either a T or a shallow Y depending on how you look at it, we bear right (Wp.13 72M) and cross the hamlet of **Kernaman**, on the far side of which, the circuit continues on a wayposted dirt track (Wp.14 76M). After a long, gentle, southerly climb toward the main ridge, we turn left at a crossroads (Wp.15 87M), at which point the 'Circuit de Mougau' is joined by the **Circuit de la Pierre Bleue**, which starts in **Commana**. When the track feeds into a lane (Wp.16 93M), we bear right, passing a major track climbing to the right 500 metres later (a possible shortcut to Wp.20 after heavy rain, when the path above the peat bog maybe waterlogged) (Wp.17 98M) before reaching the **Mougau Bihan** *allée couverte* 250 metres later (Wp.18 102M).

**Along the ridge**

Turning right on the 'Circuit des Korrigans', we traverse a peat bog via duckboards and footbridges (slippery when wet) then follow a narrow path alongside small fields to join a broad, very rough track amid banks of bracken. Turning right at a clearly wayposted junction (Wp.19 111M), we continue on another narrow path for 100 metres to a T-junction with the dirt track passed at Wp.17, at which point we leave the **Circuit des Korrigans** and turn left, staying with the 'Circuit du Mougau' (Wp.20). When the track swings left 175 metres later, we carry straight on along a narrow path (Wp.21 116M) for a brief but steady climb onto the rather flat ridge.

At the crossroads on the far side of the ridge (Wp.22 127M), we turn right and follow the main trail along the southern side of the outcrops of rock that constitute mini-summits hereabouts - the branch tracks are either firebreaks

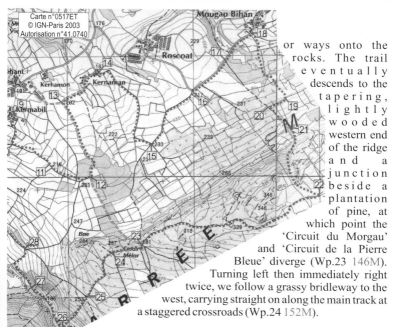

or ways onto the rocks. The trail eventually descends to the tapering, lightly wooded western end of the ridge and a junction beside a plantation of pine, at which point the 'Circuit du Morgau' and 'Circuit de la Pierre Bleue' diverge (Wp.23 146M). Turning left then immediately right twice, we follow a grassy bridleway to the west, carrying straight on along the main track at a staggered crossroads (Wp.24 152M).

When the main track swings sharp right (Wp.25 157M), we maintain direction (SW) on a minor trail descending steeply into the delightful **Vallée de l'Elorn**. Turning right (Wp.26 162M), we shadow the stream, forking right at a junction above a ford (Wp.27 168M), maintaining height as the watercourse drops away to our left. Our path then veers right, climbing back to rejoin the track left at Wp.25. Bearing left (Wp.28 174M), we traverse the hamlet of **Kerfornédic** then cross a lane (Wp.29 183M) to follow a surfaced track back to the lake (Wp.30 190M). We leave the **Circuit du Mougau** here and turn left to cross a footbridge over the **Elorn** (Wp.31 195M). 100 metres after the bridge, the path climbs away from the lake to a parking area alongside a lane (Wp.32 202M). Bearing right then forking left, we follow the main trail through the woods on the southern shore of the lake, before returning to our starting point via the dam.

# 13 BRENNILIS: THE GATES OF HELL & A GODLY LITTLE MOUNTAIN

Once dreaded by medieval pilgrims as the gateway to hell, the **Yeun Elez** peat bog at the heart of the **Monts d'Arrée** has long been tamed, first by farmers, then by government (there's a small decommissioned nuclear plant at the eastern end of the central lake), and finally by ramblers and outward bound enthusiasts.

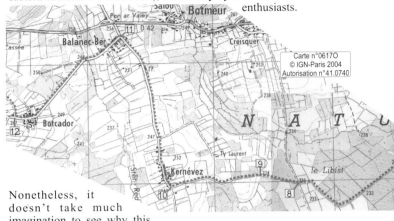

Carte n°0617O
© IGN-Paris 2004
Autorisation n°41.0740

Nonetheless, it doesn't take much imagination to see why this desolate windswept corner inspired such fear. Even nowadays, the bleak moorland has a wild and woolly look to it, and though the ways across the marsh are clearly signposted and secured by tailored paths, duckboards and pontoons, once you're in the middle of it all, there's a wonderful sense of wilderness. Add to that a fine ridge walk and the most iconic of Brittany's mini 'mountains', the **Ménez Mikel** with its starkly silhouetted chapel, and you have the makings of a superb outing.

There is, however, one substantial drawback. The walk ends with over four kilometres of road walking, unavoidable thanks to the heavily fenced government installations. The roads are quiet and not without moments of charm, nonetheless, four kilometres of tarmac is four too many, so if you can come as a two car party, do so, leaving the second vehicle at Wp.28. For those with only one vehicle, rest assured that the good bits are so very good it's worth doing the roadwalking. The only other option would be to turn left at Wp.25 then follow the outward route back to the start from Wp.10, which would be more picturesque but would bump the distance up to some thirty kilometres.

Carte n°0617O
© IGN-Paris 2004
Autorisation n°41.0740

The itinerary, which is sometimes known as the 'Tour du Lac St. Michel', combines two waymarked walks, the 'Circuit de Yeun Elez' (the 'Elez' doesn't appear on the signs) and the 'Circuit Landes & Tourbières', all major junctions of which are clearly signposted. There's little risk of drifting off path like the pilgrims used to (shrouded in mist and walking across the springy turf of the slopes, they would stray downhill and disappear in the bog), but the route is very exposed and the walk should not be undertaken when visibility is poor or rain is forecast.

5     5H     23.5km     275m     275m     2

| | |
|---|---|
| **Access:** by car | **Short Versions** |
| | (a) **Circuit de Yeun Elez** - turn left at Wp.10 to rejoin the described itinerary at Wp.25. |
| | (b) **Circuit Landes & Tourbières** - starting from Wps.10 or 14 and turning left at Wp.25. |

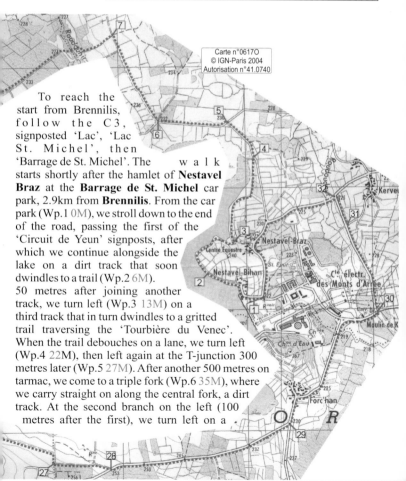

Carte n°0617O
© IGN-Paris 2004
Autorisation n°41.0740

To reach the start from Brennilis, follow the C3, signposted 'Lac', 'Lac St. Michel', then 'Barrage de St. Michel'. The walk starts shortly after the hamlet of **Nestavel Braz** at the **Barrage de St. Michel** car park, 2.9km from **Brennilis**. From the car park (Wp.1 0M), we stroll down to the end of the road, passing the first of the 'Circuit de Yeun' signposts, after which we continue alongside the lake on a dirt track that soon dwindles to a trail (Wp.2 6M).
50 metres after joining another track, we turn left (Wp.3 13M) on a third track that in turn dwindles to a gritted trail traversing the 'Tourbière du Venec'. When the trail debouches on a lane, we turn left (Wp.4 22M), then left again at the T-junction 300 metres later (Wp.5 27M). After another 500 metres on tarmac, we come to a triple fork (Wp.6 35M), where we carry straight on along the central fork, a dirt track. At the second branch on the left (100 metres after the first), we turn left on a

grassy trail leading to the 'Tourbière du Libist' (also known as **Roudouhir**) (Wp.7 46M).

The trail soon gives way to a muddy path and a series of pontoons and duckboards tracing the <u>only</u> feasible way across the marsh. Toward the end, the trail broadens to a track (at which point you may have to skirt a particularly deep puddle via the field on the right), which crosses a tiny lane a couple of minutes later (Wp.8 66M). We then pass a branch track off to the left (Wp.9 71M) and traverse more domestic countryside before reaching a T-junction with a road in the picturesque hamlet of **Kernévez** (Wp.10 81M).

We leave the 'Circuit de Yeun' here, turning right on the 'Circuit Landes & Tourbières', which follows the road for 1.4km before turning left on the road to 'Bot-cador' (Wp.11 97M).

After passing the 'Auberge des Cretes' *crêperie à la ferme* and traversing **Botcador**, we turn right on a grassy track (Wp.12 110M), which soon dwindles to a path climbing gently to a junction of the D42 and D785 at the *bar-tabac* 'La Croix Cassée' (Wp.13 120M). 75 metres up the main road (Wp.14), we turn left then immediately bear left again onto the long fell like rise of **Ménez Kador**.

**Climbing Menez Kador**

A broad well-stabilized trail snakes its way along the back of the ridge, with fine views across the lake toward our starting point and over the moorland to the west. After a long, gentle climb, we reach the rocky outcrop of **Ménez Kador** itself (Wp.15 140M), where a break is heartily recommended, particularly on the eastern side of the rocks, which give shelter from the prevailing winds. The rocky trail continues south toward the silhouette of **Ménez Mikel**, passing a minor branch off to the left (Wp.16 148M). 150 metres later, we fork right at a Y-junction (Wp.17

Carte n°0617O
© IGN-Paris 2004
Autorisation n°41.0740

150M) to cut a bend from the main trail, which we subsequently follow to the southwest toward a stand of pine and a couple of slender antenna.

After passing just to the left of the antenna, we re-cross the D42 and take a broad track (Wp.18 166M) up towards **Ménez Mikel**. Another gentle climb leads to a plateau, where we leave the main track, forking left (Wp.19 173M) on a broad, slightly boggy trail that passes just below a car-park to join a stony path climbing directly onto the summit (Wp.20 185M). The chapel is usually open if

**Menez Mikel**

**The Yeun Elez peat bog**

shelter is required. Immediately southeast of the summit, a broad path stepped with railway sleepers descends to cross the access road (Wp.21 189M). Forking left immediately after crossing the road and again 200 metres later (Wp.22 191M), we cut across the moorland to the main road, where we briefly join the **GR380/37** (Wp.23 197M).

Crossing the road, we continue on a broad dirt track to **Ty Blaise**, where the 'Circuit Landes & Tourbières' and the GR/'Circuit du Méné' divide to pass on either side of **Roc'h Cléguer** (Wp.24 206M). Either route is viable, but to minimize the road walking, we turn left, staying with the 'Landes et Tourbières' itinerary as it crosses a stand of conifer and descends toward the lake and a signposted T-junction with the 'Circuit de Yeun', which we now follow back to the start (Wp.25 213M). Turning right, we follow a narrow sandy track along the northern flank of **Roc'h Cléguer,** carrying straight on at a junction with a trail climbing to the right (Wp.26 221M). Having run dead straight for most of its course, the track eventually swings round to the right and climbs a slight rise to a second junction, where we turn left (Wp.27 240M). This track soon feeds into another, which we follow up to the right to join a back road (Wp.28 244M) - and, hopefully, a parked car!

If not, I'm afraid we now have a slightly dreary slog along the tarmac. Turning left, then left again at the T-junction 1300 metres later (Wp.29 260M), we follow the road round to the right at **Forc'han** (1.5km from Wp.28 not 2 as the sign claimed), an idyllic hamlet, despite having a disused nuclear reactor tucked into the back garden. The road eventually curves round to pass in front of a small industrial estate before reaching a junction just after the **Moulin Kerstrat** calvary (Wp.30 276M). Turning left and carrying straight on at the junction with the 'Kerveur' road (Wp.31 286M), we rejoin the C3 (Wp.32 289M), which we used to reach the start of the walk, and on which we now turn left to return to the car park.

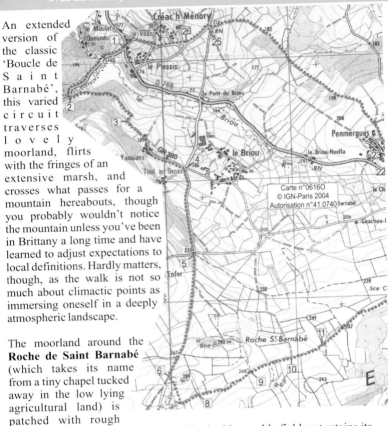

An extended version of the classic 'Boucle de Saint Barnabé', this varied circuit traverses lovely moorland, flirts with the fringes of an extensive marsh, and crosses what passes for a mountain hereabouts, though you probably wouldn't notice the mountain unless you've been in Brittany a long time and have learned to adjust expectations to local definitions. Hardly matters, though, as the walk is not so much about climactic points as immersing oneself in a deeply atmospheric landscape.

The moorland around the **Roche de Saint Barnabé** (which takes its name from a tiny chapel tucked away in the low lying agricultural land) is patched with rough pasture and the occasional rather shabby looking arable field, yet retains its original face, and is particularly appealing when swathed in swirls of twisting mist - you could easily come over all **Baskerville** here! Likewise the marsh below the **Landes de Cragou**, which is defined by a fence, but is otherwise a virtually untouched wilderness that would do very nicely for a Daphne Du Maurier moment. Despite having a couple of main roads going through it and dozens of hamlets dotted about the place, there's a wonderfully remote feeling to this region, and you probably won't meet anyone or anything you don't care to conjure up from your imagination.

**Access:** by car

Our itinerary begins to the southwest of **Le Cloître St. Thégonnec**, in the hamlet of **Le Plessis**, just north of km41 on the D769 and at the junction with the D111. There's a lay-by with room for two cars immediately south of junction, otherwise park on the sliproads accessing the hamlet of **Créac'h Ménory**. From the intersection (Wp.1 0M), we set off along the D111 toward 'Le Relecq', following the road for 550 metres. Shortly after the km21 milepost, we double back to the left (Wp.2 7M) on a dirt track tunneling into attractive woodland, passing a branch into a field on the left 150 metres later.

The track soon dwindles to a sunken path as it curves SE into agricultural land, where it joins the end of another track (Wp.3 18M).

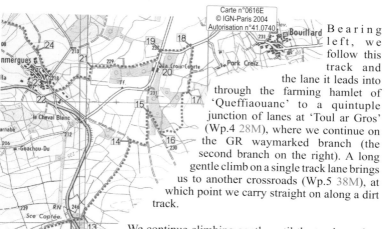

Bearing left, we follow this track and the lane it leads into through the farming hamlet of 'Queffiaouanc' to a quintuple junction of lanes at 'Toul ar Gros' (Wp.4 28M), where we continue on the GR waymarked branch (the second branch on the right). A long gentle climb on a single track lane brings us to another crossroads (Wp.5 38M), at which point we carry straight on along a dirt track.

We continue climbing gently until the track reaches the crest of a rise just short of a large electricity pylon, where there's a double turning to the left (Wp.6 54M). We take the second of the two turnings, signposted 'Circuit de Goenidou' and 'St. Barnabé', heading SE to a T-junction, where we again turn left (Wp.7 57M) carrying straight on at the junction 125 metres later (Wp.8 59M). We now simply follow this track along the crest, carrying straight on at three successive junctions, the first a signposted branch on the left (Wp.9 64M) to the 'Roche de St. Barnabé', the second an intersection with a major farm track (Wp.10 71M), the third a turning off to the right (Wp.11 75M).

At the end of the track, we cross the D769 (Wp.12 85M) and traverse a stand of pine, immediately after which, we leave the 'Circuit de Goenidou' and fork left on the brown 'VTT' itinerary (Wp.13). Initially a grassy trail running alongside a field, the VTT (mountain bike) route soon traverses open moorland then dwindles to a delightful but intermittently waterlogged sunken path.

**The VTT trail after Wp.13**

At a wayposted, slanting T-junction, we bear right (Wp.14 98M) (ESE) then veer north as the trail broadens to a waterlogged track.

When this feeds into a broader, better stabilised track (Wp.15 103M), we briefly leave the 'Boucle de St.Barnabé', doubling back to the right then turning left 100 metres later into the 'Reserve Biologique des Landes de Cragou' (Wp.16 105M).

**The bird-watching hide**

After crossing a ladder stile, our path weaves alongside an electric fence delineating the reserve, eventually reaching a stand of oak and a bird-watching hide (Wp.17 113M). From the hide, a farm track leads up to the lane accessing the hamlet of **Bouillard** (Wp.18 118M), on which we turn left.

Turning left again at the T-junction above **La Croix Courte** (Wp.19 121M), then right 40 metres later on a dirt track signposted 'Circuit VTT N2' (Wp.20), we rejoin the classic **Boucle de St. Barnabé**.

After 250 metres, the track dwindles to a trail that joins the end of another track at the entrance to a field (Wp.21 129M). Turning left, we follow this track to the hamlet of **Penmergues**, where we turn right (Wp.22 134M). After 75 metres (Wp.23), we fork right then immediately left, on a farm track that's surfaced for the first 100 metres. Ignoring a turning off to the right 150 metres later (Wp.24), we follow the main track as it curves NW, and descends amid attractive pasture and coppicing.

The track eventually bottoms out at a confluence of rivulets (prone to flooding in winter), from where we climb to a junction of lanes below **Le Cloître St. Thégonnec** (Wp.25 161M). We bear left on the main lane, then fork right 100 metres later onto the lower of the two roads into **Créach Ménory** (Wp.26), after which we simply keep on descending at each junction to return to the start.

# 15 HUELGOAT: FINISTÈRE'S LEGENDARY FOREST

Nestling in the heart of **Finistère**, the forest of **Huelgoat** is one of two extensive woodland areas that have become associated with the Breton Arthurian tradition. It's a lovely wood and there are countless walks to be done, many already integrated into waymarked circuits. The present itinerary, a variant on the **Circuit des Chevreuils** (roe deer), serves as a good introduction both to the less famous corners of the forest and to several other itineraries. It's well waymarked and clearly signposted throughout, and as long as you take note of the change in signposting at Wp.15 can be done without having your nose buried in the book.

**Access:** by car

We start from the roadside car-park below the 'Maison Forestière de l'Arquellen', which lies a little over a kilometre to the east of **Huelgoat** village centre on the D769a. From the car-park (Wp.1 0M), we take the 'Circuit des Chevreuils' track to the north, climbing amid attractive moss clad woodland before turning right for the 'Café-Librairie L'Autre Rive' (Wp.2 6M).

After passing an attractive spring, our trail emerges on an asphalt lane in front of the *café-librairie* (the only refreshment en route, but well worth a visit for morning coffee or a snack after the walk) at the hamlet of **Restidiou Braz** (Wp.3 12M). Turning left, we follow the lane through **Restidiou Bihan**, passing the first signposted intersection with the 'Circuit de Menhir' (Wp.4 21M). We bear left at the junction 200 metres later (Wp.5 22M) then fork right 150 metres after that on a dirt track, signposted for both the 'Circuit des Chevreuils' and the 'Circuit de Grande Lande' (Wp.6).

**On the main forest track**

The track traverses rising woodland and heath, on the far side of which we stay on the same track at a crossroads (Wp.7 32M). We then climb a second rise and, just before the next descent, double back to the left on a clearly signposted sunken path tunneling into the woods (Wp.8 37M). Rejoining the 'Circuit de Menhir' at a T-junction, we turn right (Wp.9 42M) and climb along an airy bridleway. Immediately after passing a minor branch forking off to the right (Wp.10), we turn left at a T-junction with a dirt track (Wp.11 46M). Bearing right at the next junction (Wp.12 48M), we descend below an elaborate hen coop to the end of a lane at the farm hamlet of **Brignou**, where

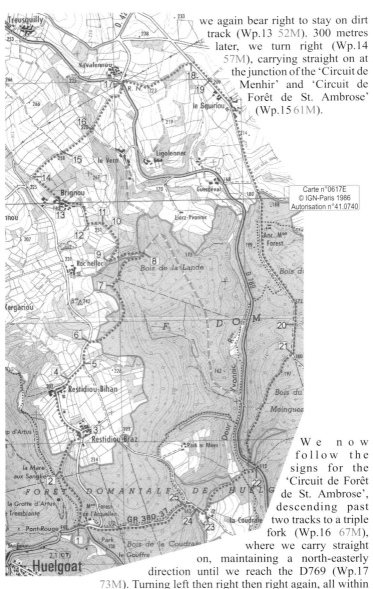

we again bear right to stay on dirt track (Wp.13 52M). 300 metres later, we turn right (Wp.14 57M), carrying straight on at the junction of the 'Circuit de Menhir' and 'Circuit de Forêt de St. Ambrose' (Wp.15 61M).

We now follow the signs for the 'Circuit de Forêt de St. Ambrose', descending past two tracks to a triple fork (Wp.16 67M), where we carry straight on, maintaining a north-easterly direction until we reach the D769 (Wp.17 73M). Turning left then right then right again, all within the space of 50 metres, we follow a grassy trail back toward the woods. When the trail joins a lane, we turn right (Wp.18 82M). 250 metres later, the 'Circuit de Forêt de St. Ambrose' branches off to the left and discrete signposting for the 'Circuit des Chevreuils' resumes (Wp.19 86M). We carry straight on, following the road for another kilometre through the hamlet of **Squiriou**, back to the official 'Forêt Domaniale de Huelgoat', where we join the **GR380** (at the perimeter of the woods, not further on as indicated on the IGN map) and the asphalt gives way to a roughly metalled track.

The track passes a forestry house and a junction with another major track running in from the left (Wp.20 106M), 275 metres after which, we briefly leave the **Circuit des Chevreuils** and fork right (Wp.21 110M), following the GR as it curves through sweeping birch and beech woodland back to the D769.

**The ford after Wp.22**

50 metres to the left, we rejoin the 'Circuit des Chevreuils' (Wp.22 124M) on a track descending SE to ford a stream (there's a rather weary footbridge on the right) before climbing to a lane (Wp.23 133M). Turning right, we ignore the first turning on the left (Wp.24), which is followed by the GR (again contrary to what the IGN map suggests) and continue on the lane as it rounds a bend, where we turn left on a bowery track signposted 'Circuit de l'Arquellen'/'Circuit des Chevreuils' (Wp.25 135M), which leads back to the **Restidiou Braz** road and the start of the itinerary.

# 16 HUELGOAT REGAINED: SIGHTSEEING

When this book was planned, I only intended doing one walk in **Huelgoat**, but it's such a fine forest I felt compelled to return a second time a fortnight later, which is about as high a recommendation as I can make. The present itinerary is designed to visit the forest's more famous tourist attractions, but it's also another excellent introductory route for those wishing to venture further afield, encompassing as it does numerous waymarked routes plus a host of minor paths ripe for additional exploration.

**Strolls** - see Wp.6

**Access:** on foot from **Huelgoat**.

The canal feeding the mine

We start from the large municipal car-park behind the town hall, signposted 'Mairie' throughout the village of **Huelgoat**. Directly behind the *Mairie*, a walled alley (signposted 'Ancien Mine') descends to a narrow canal, where we turn right, as indicated by yellow waymarks (Wp.1 0M). We follow the canal and the 'Circuit de Ancien Mine' to the D769 (Wp.2 6M), where we turn left, forking right 75 metres later to continue along the canal (Wp.3).

We stick with the canal as it traverses deepening, darkening woodland, twice crossing the 'Circuit de Arquellen' (Wp.4 13M & Wp.5 18M). The bridge (Wp.6 29M) after the second intersection would make a suitable turning point for a stroll, otherwise we continue along the canal until it reaches a small hydroelectric plant and reservoir (Wp.7 42M), where we leave the 'Circuit de Ancien Mine'. After crossing the grid bridge behind the reservoir, we take a path descending to the left, signposted 'La Mine'. At the next junction, this path joins the 'Circuit de Arquellen' (Wp.8 45M), which we follow down across a dry canal until it runs into the broad bare scar of the former mine works. After fording a shallow brook

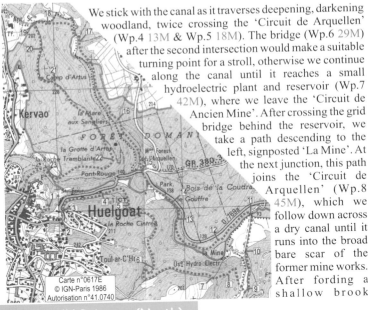

Carte n°0617E
© IGN-Paris 1986
Autorisation n°41.0740

bisecting the mining area, we follow the 'Circuit de Arquellen' to the north along a broad track (Wp.9 48M). Maintaining direction (N) at a slanting T-junction (Wp.10 53M), we soon cross a bridge over the **Rivière d'Argent**, immediately after which we turn left, to follow the **GR37** along the northern flank of the river (Wp.11 57M). After climbing away from the watercourse, we turn left at a T-junction (Wp.12 65M) and descend back to the banks of the river, where we pass **La Mare aux Fées** (the Fairies' Pond) (Wp.13 72M) before climbing alongside a spectacular chaos of rock.

Five minutes later, we pass a junction with a signposted path climbing to the left ('Belvedere / Stelle Victor Segalen'), after which we reach a glorious chasm (**Le Gouffre**), where the watercourse is submerged in massive rocks. Just above **Le Gouffre**, we rejoin the D769 (Wp.14 78M).

**The first chaos**

Turning left, we follow the road for nearly 400 metres, passing a car-park and a lay-by. At the **Maison Forestière de l'Arquellen** car-park (the start of Walk 15), we take the broad trail of the 'Circuit des Chevreuils' to the north (Wp.15 84M). When the 'Circuit des Chevreuils' forks off to the right, we continue along the main trail (Wp.16 90M), passing above **La Mare aux Sangliers** ('The Wild Boars' Pond'), a pleasant paddling pool on a hot day.

We ignore the next two turnings (on the right to 'Restidiou Bihan' and on the left to 'Pont Gwern' - not waymarked due to poor GPS reception) and continue along the main trail for 'Camp d'Artus'. The path narrows and becomes shadier as it approaches a signposted junction where the 'Circuit de Menhir' bears right (Wp.17 104M). We fork left here then left again almost immediately to cross a narrow stone bridge, beyond which we follow a sunken path that climbs steadily to a wooded plateau. We maintain direction (W) at a crossroads (Wp.18 112M), then turn left at a major confluence of tracks to follow the 'Sentier de Camp d'Artus' (Wp.19 114M). The track leads to an explanatory panel at the site of the **Camp d'Artus**, a Celtic hill fort, where we fork right (Wp.20 117M) on a minor trail that passes a couple of viewing platforms before rejoining the main track (Wp.21 125M). Turning right, we follow the main track until it descends to a signposted junction above the 'Grotte d'Artus', at which point we turn right on the 'Sentier des Amoureux' (Wp.22 139M).

The **Sentier des Amoureux** descends steeply to the cluster of natural monuments (Wp.23 148M) that lure so many tourists to **Huelgoat**, notably the **Roche Tremblante** (a 137 ton boulder that can, in theory, be rocked by hand), the **Ménage de la Vierge** (erosion scars said to resemble the Virgin's chattels) and the **Chaos du Moulin**. After visiting the sights (not counted in subsequent timings), we climb alongside the chaos and follow the well-trodden tourist trail past the raked seats of the open air **Théâtre de Verdure** and through the rocks back to the lakeside road on the edge of the village. The village square and *mairie* car-park are reached by following the road round to the left.

Glance at a sketch map of the **Parc Naturel d'Armorique** and you'll see that **Guerlesquin** is an annex to the main park, a sort of satellite that seems to have been tacked on as an afterthought. Yet in many ways it's anything but peripheral and is as central to the park's identity as places nearer its geographical heart. The town itself is charming and the rolling countryside surrounding it, laced with streams and tracks and sunken paths, and spotted with thickets, coppices, wild little woods and abandoned hamlets, virtually merits national park status in its own right. We follow the **GR380** until Wp.20, but after that waymarking is ancient and frequently invisible, so I'm afraid a certain amount of time consulting the book is necessary. Mud is virtually guaranteed on the farm tracks.

**Access:** on foot from **Guerlesquin**.

**Strolls/Short Version**

There's a maze of trails in the **Coat Haouden** woods (access via Wp.28) that merit further exploration.

Carte n°0616E
© IGN-Paris 2004
Autorisation n°41.0740

From the 'Place du Martray' car-park in front of **Guerlesquin** church (Wp.1 0M), we descend along 'Rue du General de Gaulle' (signposted 'Plan d'eau'/'Camping') and its continuation as 'Rue de Ewen Gwen', then take 'Rue de Kernaman' (Wp.2 4M) i.e. turn left then immediately bear right as indicated by a GR waymark. At the far end of this residential road, we cross 'Rue de la Residence' (Wp.3 10M) and follow a lane down to the **Etang du Guic**, where we turn right (Wp.4 15M). When the shoreside lane joins the D42, we cross the main road onto a grassy bridleway (Wp.5 20M).

The bridleway tunnels through attractive mixed woodland before broadening to a muddy track defined by a coppice

**Etang du Guic**

hedgerow. At the **Ménez Riou** farm, the track runs into a lane, 50 metres along which, we bear right on another, narrower track (Wp.6 38M). Carrying straight on at a crossroads of trails 200 metres later (Wp.7), we follow the track until it emerges on a broad but little used backroad (Wp.8 48M), where we turn left.

**... sunken path ...**

We climb steadily to steeply for 400 metres until the road levels out at a junction, 175 metres after which, we turn right on the 'Kergolet' access road (Wp.9 60M), which continues as a dirt track after the farmhouse 75 metres later. Turning left at the first junction (Wp.10 69M) then right on the **Kervretell** access lane (Wp.11 72M), we pass the entrances to various farm buildings and cottages. After the farm, the lane becomes a dirt track again and we fork right at a Y-junction (Wp.12 76M), carrying straight on at the next junction (Wp.13 80M) then immediately forking left to follow the path rather than the track running parallel to it. This idyllic sunken path, the first of many that characterize the rest of this itinerary, descends by easy stages through a beech wood back into the **Vallée du Guic**, crossing the stream via a footbridge (Wp.14 90M) in front of the equally idyllic **Kergariou** mill cottage.

Our itinerary continues on a dirt track that climbs gently away from the mill then levels out before reaching the **Kergariou** farm hamlet (Wp.15 101M). 25 metres before the farm lane, we turn right on a rougher, rockier track climbing gently to cross a small rise before rejoining the D42 (Wp.16 110M). Turning right, we follow the road for 200 metres then take the second turning on the left, a track descending past a small house with blue shutters (Wp.17 115M). The track descends through an alley of conifers to a field-side path where we bear right (Wp.18 118M). The path doglegs round the field and descends into a valley where it becomes a narrow dirt track burrowing through the woods to join a much broader track (Wp.19 127M). Bearing left, we ford a rivulet and climb to a tiny lane (Wp.20 132M).

One of the sunken paths

At this point <u>we leave the GR</u> and turn right, following the road for 500 metres. When the lane swings sharp left at the entrance to the **Keraël** manor house, we carry straight on along an unmarked grassy track (Wp.21 140M), forking left at the Y-junction 50 metres later (Wp.22). On the far side of the abandoned hamlet of **Quélennec**, 25 metres along the access lane, we turn right (Wp.23 147M) on another sunken path descending to a Y-junction, where we bear right (Wp.24 152M), crossing another tiny stream and climbing to the **Tromolouarn** farm buildings.

Immediately after the farm, we turn right (Wp.25 157M) on yet another sunken path descending to (you've guessed it!) another stream, which we follow to the right for 50 metres to reach a rather rickety footbridge, 50 metres after which, we fork left (Wp.26 160M). Climbing steeply on a path so sunken it's virtually dejected (you won't be; it's lovely), we reach a slanting T-junction with a broader trail, at which point we bear right (Wp.27 168M).

After a final brief climb, the trail levels out alongside fields then veers round to join a dirt track leading to a minor road (Wp.28 176M) where we again bear right. Bearing left at the next junction (Wp.29 180M) and carrying straight on at the 'Keravel' roundabout (Wp.30 190M), we follow this lane back to the centre of **Guerlesquin**.

One of the finest bits of coast on a very fine coast, this mini-rollercoaster ride is a joy from beginning to end, with fabulous sea views, abundant and varied vegetation, and enough fresh air to put Airwick out of business. It's particularly appealing on a summer's evening when the slanting rays of the low lying sun bathe the coast in a beautiful golden light.

**A rollercoaster ride**

There's a very slight risk of vertigo and some care is required if walking with children or when the path is wet.

4 | 3H | 10.5km | 200m / 200m | ! | ↻ | 5*

* Most notably, **Hotel de la Baie** in **Loquémeau**. Alternatively, for something a bit different, try the excellent **Les Terrasses du Yaudet** tea house at **Le Yaudet**, just north of **Loquémeau**.

**Access:** on foot from **Trédrez** or **Loquémeau**.

> **Short Versions**
> Signposted alternatives are passed at Wps.6 & 7.

From the 'Ecole de Voile'/kayak rental stand behind **Pointe de Séhar** at **Port de Loquémeau** (Wp.1 0M), we take the GR signposted track curving behind the **Etang de Vorlen** until we come to a triple fork (Wp.2 5M). Ignoring the bridleway climbing to the left, we fork right along the coastal path proper, staying on the GR for another 500 metres. After passing two houses, we turn left at a clear, signposted turning, leaving the GR to climb steeply on the 'Circuit de Falaises PR de Trédrez' (Wp.3 14M).

When the path reaches a staggered junction, we turn right twice (Wp.4 17M) and follow a fine trail lined with elder, sloe, brambles and bracken, enjoying excellent views along the coast to the south, including the broad expanse of the **Grève de St. Michel** sand flats, the site of horse-races, sand-dinghy regattas, and sheets of nitrate fuelled seaweed. The path runs into a track that immediately joins a lane, where we again turn right twice, as indicated by an abundance of waymarking (Wp.5 30M).

After passing the hamlet of **Lann-Charlez**, we come to a junction of lanes and a variant of the **GR34B** (Wp.6 37M). Bearing left then immediately turning right, we follow a dirt track (not a road as some maps suggest) that eventually curves southwest to another signposted junction (Wp.7 45M), where we leave the 'Falaises de Trédrez' PR and turn left on the 'PR en dominant St.-Michel-en-Grève'. Maintaining direction (SE) at the next junction 100 metres later (Wp.8), we head toward the church spire at **Trédrez**.

On the edge of the village, our track becomes a lane (Wp.9 56M), which in turn joins the main road through **Trédrez** (Wp.10 58M). Turning right, we ignore the GR waymarks in front of the *bar-crêperie* and stroll past the lovely little church (well worth visiting), before forking left at the Y-junction to the south of the village and immediately taking the track on the right (Wp.11 60M). The track dwindles to an alley leading to a junction with a lane, where we turn right (Wp.12 68M) then, as indicated by waymarks, right again fifty metres later on a bowery path that soon drops down to a junction at the end of the lane (Wp.13 72M).

**Trédrez church**

Sticking with the waymarked route, we climb steadily through the woods on a path that widens to a drive shortly before joining another lane, where we turn right (Wp.14 76M). At the 'Beg ar Forn' calvary, we turn left (Wp.15 79M) then left again 175 metres later (Wp.16 83M) on a sunken path that descends through a lovely long tunnel of vegetation (watch you head, there's some low hanging boughs) to join the coastal path (Wp.17 94M). Turn right and enjoy!

The coastal path passes another path feeding in from the right 150 metres later (Wp.18), shortly after which we round the lip of the bay and see the remainder of the walk stretching away ahead of us. After passing a couple of short, slightly vertiginous sections, the path is either wide or well sheltered by the coastward embankment as it approaches a first stand of pine - a good place for a picnic. Thereafter, we pass three paths climbing to the right (Wp.19 112M, Wp.20 133M, and Wp.21 148M) before rejoining our outward route at Wp.3 (165M).

Choked with a superfluity of posh villas, grand hotels and bijoux apartment blocks, and subject to an alarming influx of traffic on summer weekends, the ever popular **Côte de Granite** Rose may not seem like a very promising walking environment, but the coast really is very spectacular (rich people do not, on the whole, gather in dowdy locations), an extraordinary scattering of pink rock spattered about the azure blue sea with all the verve, dash, instinctive artistry and chaotic serendipity of a child's first painting.

**Castel Menguy**

Add a fine chestnut wood, some beautiful beaches, and some enviably located restaurants, and you have all that's required for a great day out.

**Access:** on foot from **Trestraou**.

> **Stroll**
> **St. Guirec** from the car park at Wp.20

\* Haven't tried them, but if only for location, the restaurants in **Port de Ploumanac'h** and at **Plage de St. Guirec** merit a high star rating.

From the large blue 'Gare Maritime' sign at the western end of **Plage de Trestraou** (Wp.1 0M), we follow 'Rue de la Clarte' up to the first bend then continue along the GR behind 'Residence La Roseraie' (Wp.2) following a pedestrian alley that dwindles to a path after a couple of minutes. 650 metres later, we leave the coastal path and climb to the left on a broad trail signposted 'Les Sentiers de Ploumanach' (Wp.3 15M). Maintaining direction (SW) at the staggered crossroads of lane, track, and path (Wp.4 18M), we follow a path up to the D788, where we cross directly onto 'Rue des Glycines' (Wp.5 22M).

At the far end of **Rue des Glycines**, we turn right (Wp.6 24M), toward the attractive little sailors' chapel of **La Clarte**, beyond which we pick up another path at the far end of the car park, also indicated by a 'Sentiers de Ploumanach' sign (Wp.7 28M). When the path emerges on the road, we turn left (Wp.8 30M), then right (Wp.9 32M) and follow 'Rue des Carrieres' down past the quarries toward the 'Vallée des Traouiero', where we turn right on the 'Chemin Roland Fick' dirt track (Wp.10 37M).

The track narrows to a grassy trail that in turn gives way to a path burrowing into a lovely chestnut wood. Following a waymarked 'VTT'/mountain bike route, we turn left at a T-junction (Wp.11 48M) then right when the path emerges on a road (Wp.12 52M).

Port de Ploumanac'h

50 metres before the T-junction with the main road, we turn left (Wp.13 57M) and descend to **Port de Ploumanac'h**, where we rejoin the GR, which we follow back to the start.

**Approaching Plage de St. Guirec**

After contouring round the harbour, we take 'Chemin de la Pointe' (Wp.14 73M) then turn right in front of the '7 Îles' embarkation point (Wp.15 77M).

The path across the ensuing headland is an absolute delight and an absolute maze. Essentially, if you just want to get on, keep bearing right on the main trail. If you want to enjoy yourself, keep turning left. They're all dead ends and all lead somewhere spectacular.

Carte n°0714OT
© IGN-Paris 1996
Autorisation n°41.0740

St. Guirec

Having negotiated this maze (it only actually takes about five minutes, but will probably fill twenty), we emerge on the exquisite **Plage de St. Guirec**, at the far end of which (Wp.16 98M), we take the 'Passage Jean Laborey' across the next headland, passing a celebrated diabolic garage and the lighthouse (Wp.17 106M).

We carry straight on at the triple junction after the lifeboat house (Wp.18 112M) before bearing south toward the radar station, below which we pass a car park (Wp.19 128M). We rejoin our outward route at Wp.3 (139M).

Despite its dramatic title, this is a relatively easy coastal walk, level for the most part, but borrowing drama from the fabulous seascape. 'Hell' is the **Baie d'Enfer** where we first join the *sentier cotier*, 'low water'a hint that the itinerary should be done on a falling tide, not because the path is prone to flooding, but because the retreating water reveals an extraordinary chaos of rock and mini-islands, many with houses on them, that edge the peninsula like an elaborate frame of filigree.

**The house between the rocks**

The highlight of the walk is Brittany's most famous house, a tiny cottage sandwiched between two massive rocks shielding it from the sea. Not so long ago, it was the home of a poverty-stricken seaweed gatherer, who might have been the richest woman in Brittany had she enjoyed anticipatory royalties on all the postcards that have been sold of the place.

Nowadays, its fame can mean the headland gets a little crowded at weekends, but it's no less extraordinary for that, and anyone who doesn't fancy the full itinerary is strongly recommended to do the stroll.

* at Wp.1)

**Access:** by car

| **Stroll** |
| --- |
| **Kericu** (Wp.23) to **Pointe du Château** (see Wp.24), and **Le Gouffre** (see Wp.26), returning the same way. |

To reach the start, take the D31 out of **Plougrescant**. 1.9km from the junction with the D8, turn right for 'Goeurmel' 'Roudour' and follow the lane down to the hamlet of **Kermerrien** and the 'Goeurmel' car park. From the car park (Wp.1 0M), we stroll back up the lane into **Kermerrien** and fork left at the first bend on a waymarked bridleway (Wp.2 3M). The bridleway climbs steadily then broadens to a track beside a couple of bungalows, beyond which we carry straight on at a junction on the U-bend of another track (Wp.3 12M).

When the track joins a lane at 'Keraniou'(Wp.4 16M), we turn right, then left 200 metres later on a yellow waymarked track that leaves the road immediately before the **Le Palais** farmhouse (Wp.5 18M). A little over 500 metres later, we cross the D31 (Wp.6 27M) then turn left 250 metres after that, following the 'Circuit de Gouermel en Plougrescant' (Wp.7 31M). The track leads to a lane, where we bear left (Wp.8 40M) then turn right 125 metres later

(Wp.9 42M). At the junction with the D8, we turn right (Wp.10 45M), then left after 200 metres on the 'Roche Jaune' lane (Wp.11 48M).

The lane snakes through a chicane, immediately after which we turn left (Wp.12 50M), descending a couple of rough steps onto a sunken path leading to the delightful **Ruisseau de Lizildry**.

Turning right at the stream (Wp.13 55M) and staying on the right bank, we stroll down the lovely, lightly wooded valley, following the main path as it climbs away from the stream and becomes a broad grassy track heading back toward the **Roche Jaune** lane.

Lizildry Valley

Just short of the lane (Wp.14 68M), we double back to the left past a spring and *lavoir*, once again on a fine sunken path descending through mixed woodland.

When the path curves round to a Y-junction, we fork left (Wp.15 75M) and continue winding along the southern flank of the valley, passing another major path coming in from the right (Wp.16 81M) before descending to a lane beside the 'Moulin d'Arere' (Wp.17 86M).

We turn left here then immediately right to join the GR/*sentier cotier*, which we simply follow all the way round the peninsula back to our starting point. There's really no call for reading a description of this, as it's a very straightforward, easy path, and is well waymarked throughout. The only points at which there is even minimal scope for confusion are at Wps.21 / 24 / 25 / & 30. Otherwise, everything that ensues is simply for the purposes of pacing progress or for indicating other access points for GPS enthusiasts.

- After 10 minutes, the GR bears right at some very explicit 'Propriete Privé' signs and follows a fieldside path before momentarily dipping onto a beach. Curving round the marshy harbour of **Beg ar Vilin**, it runs into a lane, where we bear left then immediately turn right for 'Pors Hir', recovering the path beyond the oyster packing plant (Wp.18 115M).

- After crossing the car park below the hamlet of **Castel**, we recover the coastal path as it passes behind an intriguing outhouse/dovecot (Wp.19 124M).

- We then cross the end of a lane below the hamlet of **Kerbleustic** (Wp.20 134M).

- After veering away from the coast to protect the **Crec'h Bleiz** haven from erosion, the GR joins a lane and we turn right (Wp.21 146M) to descend back to the coast and the *sentier cotier* (Wp.22 153M).

- Shortly after forking left off the driveway to a private house (Wp.23 158M), we reach a slightly obscure junction amid a small stand of pine (Wp.24 160M). For views out to sea and across the northernmost chaos of rocks, bear right onto the **Pointe du Château** then retrace your steps to the stand of pine. To continue on the main walk, we turn left.

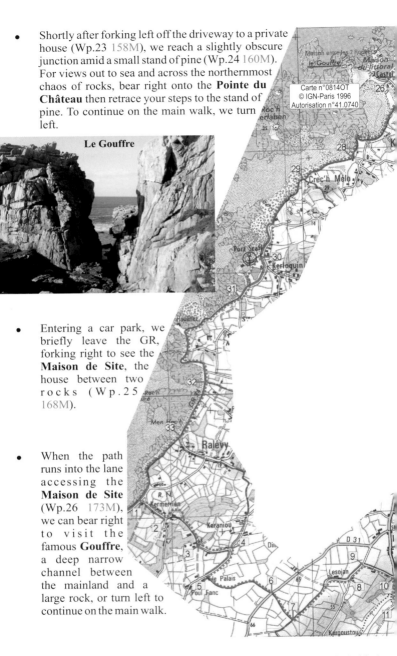

Le Gouffre

- Entering a car park, we briefly leave the GR, forking right to see the **Maison de Site**, the house between two rocks (Wp.25 168M).

- When the path runs into the lane accessing the **Maison de Site** (Wp.26 173M), we can bear right to visit the famous **Gouffre**, a deep narrow channel between the mainland and a large rock, or turn left to continue on the main walk.

- The lane joins the main road round the headland and we turn right behind the first cottage on the right, recovering the footpath (Wp.27 175M).

- After doglegging round headland house N°1, the GR joins a dirt track (Wp.28 187M), which soon leads into a broad trail passing a signposted turning for the 'Circuit de Pors Scaff' (Wp.29 193M).

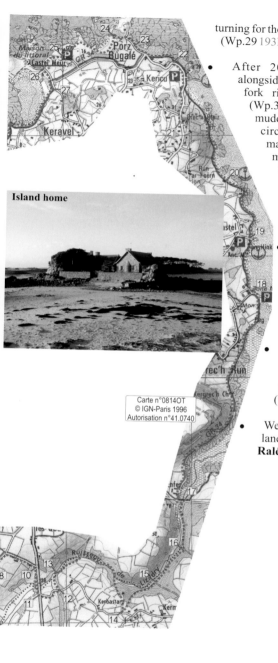

Island home

- After 200 metres walking alongside the coastal lane, we fork right toward a house (Wp.30 203M) and follow a muddy *'sentier cotier'* path circumscribing a small marsh (NB if this is too muddy, stay on the lane for 75 metres, then bear right on the branch lane, the official route of the GR).

- 150 metres later, the GR and *sentier cotier* rejoin along a shallow pebbly dike (Wp.31 209M).

- After 50 metres on a stabilized track, we carry straight on along the path (Wp.32 225M).

- We cross the end of a lane below the hamlet of **Ralévy** (Wp.33 231M).

Carte n°0814OT
© IGN-Paris 1996
Autorisation n°41.0740

... a leafy embrasure ...

An estuary walk with a difference in that the greater part of the coastal path winds through wonderfully varied woodland so that the deep blue sea views are embellished by a leafy embrasure and laced with a craquelure of spindly branches.

The outward leg is well waymarked and obvious so long as you're not confused by occasional junctions where the GR veers inland to avoid a stretch of the old path now subject to erosion.

The return via the hinterland is less interesting than the coastal path and involves a fair amount of tarmac, some of which maybe busy during the summer, which is why we opted to do the best bit first in case you wish to adapt the itinerary as a linear route. If you have the option of coming as a two car party, the outward leg would make a lovely one-way walk.

| 3 | 4¾ H | 12.75km | 175m / 175m | ↻ | 4 |

**Access:** by car

### Strolls
As is often the case, the coastal path is accessible via several minor roads, making it ideal of linear strolls, notably Wps. 1-7 / 7-9 / 9-11 / & 14-11

We start 100 metres west of the chapel in the village of **Kergrist** (signposted 'Paimpol par Kergrist' on the D786 just east of the bridge over the **River Trieux**) where an unnamed lane debouches on the secondary road and there's space to park on either side of the junction. Directly opposite the lane, we take the clearly waymarked **GR34** (Wp.1 0M), which descends via a broad grassy trail to the village *lavoir* (Wp.2 3M), where we turn left.

Our path descends towards the banks of the broadening river, passing a waymarked variant of the GR climbing to the right (Wp.3 9M), after which there's no call to be looking at the book until we reach **Loguivy**, as we simply follow the clearly waymarked GR all the way along the estuary until it curves round toward the port.

**Descending towards the estuary**

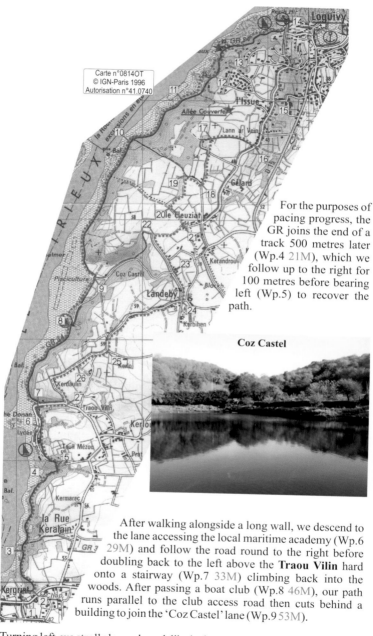

Carte n°0814OT
© IGN-Paris 1996
Autorisation n°41.0740

For the purposes of pacing progress, the GR joins the end of a track 500 metres later (Wp.4 21M), which we follow up to the right for 100 metres before bearing left (Wp.5) to recover the path.

**Coz Castel**

After walking alongside a long wall, we descend to the lane accessing the local maritime academy (Wp.6 29M) and follow the road round to the right before doubling back to the left above the **Traou Vilin** hard onto a stairway (Wp.7 33M) climbing back into the woods. After passing a boat club (Wp.8 46M), our path runs parallel to the club access road then cuts behind a building to join the 'Coz Castel' lane (Wp.9 53M).

Turning left, we stroll along a broad dike before recovering the woodland path between a private house and a summer cabin.

Staying on the coastal path at the next two junctions (Wp.10 74M & Wp.11 86M), we reach our first steep climb behind a large outcrop of rock, above

**... remarkable stand of strawberry trees ...**

which we turn left (Wp.12 91M), descending back to the shore amid a remarkable stand of strawberry trees.

A mini-rollercoaster ensues, taking us behind **La Roche aux Oiseaux** to a multiple junction in a glade of conifer, where we bear left (Wp.13 103M), back down to the shore for the final approach to **Loguivy**.

The coastal path climbs to the end of a lane on the fringes of **Loguivy** (Wp.14 113M), where we turn right, leaving the GR and heading inland. If you want refreshments, either stay on the GR as it curves round to the port or take the first turning on the left. Out of season, the only places liable to be open are the *auberge* and the pizzeria; the welcome is considerably warmer in the latter - and the pizzas aren't half bad, either! Otherwise, simply follow the lane inland, carrying straight on at the 'Rue de l'Issue' crossroads (Wp.15 121M). 100 metres after a signposted turning directing 'Paimpol' traffic down to the left, we leave the lane, turning right on a surfaced track accessing the houses in the middle of the hamlet of **Lann ar Veïn** (Wp.16 130M).

The asphalt almost immediately gives way to a grassy trail traversing agricultural fields, on the far side of which we turn left on a dirt track passing in front of cabin N°1 (Wp.17 136M). After maintaining a southerly direction on the lane the track feeds into, we take the first turning on the right (Wp.18 142M), then turn left 100 metres later on an unmarked, grassy track (Wp.19). When this track reaches a T-junction, we turn left (Wp.20 153M) then right 150 metres later, just before the **Le Cleuziat** farmhouse, on a grassy sunken trail (Wp.21 156M).

The trail joins a partially surfaced track, at which point we turn left (Wp.22 159M), maintaining direction (SE) when the track becomes a lane. Carrying straight on at the 'Coz Castel' turning (Wp.23 162M), we reach the hamlet of **Landeby**, where we turn right, still on tarmac, for 'Kerlo' (Wp.24 166M). 750 metres after **Landeby**, we bear right on a narrow, surfaced track (Wp.25 174M), ignoring a fork on the left 50 metres later. At a junction with a second broad track on the left (Wp.26 178M), we carry straight on along the surfaced track. We then dogleg round the restored **Kerdaulin** farmhouse and descend to the **Traou Vilin** road (Wp.27 184M), a couple of hundred metres above Wp.7, from where we follow our outward route back to the start.

At once a satellite suburb of **St. Brieuc** and a tourist town with no less than three campsites, **Pordic** should be built up to within an inch of its life, certainly to within an inch of its coast, which is why this walk comes as such a pleasant surprise. Traversing heath covered cliffs tumbling into the clear blue sea and skirting some beautiful black beaches tucked into hidden coves (the best of which are only accessible on foot), this is a lovely stretch of the coastal path that's well worth the detour if you happen to be passing on the nearby express way. Don't be alarmed by all the 'villes' on the map, this is not a cluster of towns. In the one time gallo-speaking half of Brittany, *ville* indicates a hamlet.

* There are several bars and restaurants in **Pordic**, but all were closed when we visited.

**Access:** by car or bus
(Line 9 **Pordic-Champ de Mars**).

### Short Version
**Vau Madec** *sentier de decouverte* - follow the end of the walk in reverse to Wp.11 then turn right to reach Wp.18.

### Strolls
As a glance at the map will indicate, anyone staying in the vicinity of **Pordic** can reach just about any point on this walk, whether on foot, by bike or car, via the lanes that form a starburst round the town centre.

We start from the bus stop opposite the chapel at the hamlet of **La Croix Guingard** (Wp.1 0M). If arriving by car, from the centre of **Pordic** follow the signs for 'Campings' then 'Le Roc de l'Hervieu' to

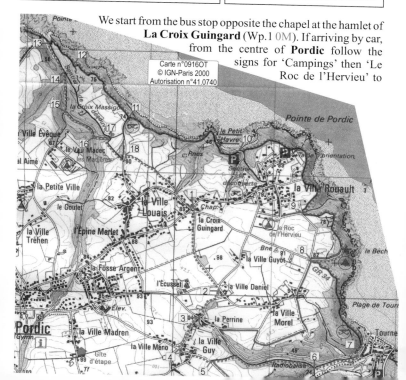

Carte n°0916OT
© IGN-Paris 2000
Autorisation n°41.0740

the 'Rue Surcouf'/'Rue Duguay Trouin' crossroads, where there's a small parking area. From the crossroads, we take the unmarked road passing in front of the chapel then immediately turn right on 'Rue de Cotenti', leaving the built up area and traversing large arable fields. We carry straight on at the calvary crossroads 700 metres later then immediately turn right on 'Rue de Guivaux' (Wp.2 10M) and follow the road round the pond.

At the hamlet of **La Perrine** (Wp.3 14M), we carry straight on past the bus stop then take the first turning on the left (Wp.4 17M), 75 metres after which the road gives way to a dirt track in front of a farmhouse. 100 metres after that, we turn left on a branch track (Wp.5 20M) that descends into the valley below the **Plage de Tournemine** road. At the bottom of the valley, when the trail joins a broader track, we turn left (Wp.6 30M) then cross the **Tournemine** road and immediately fork left on the **GR34** for 'Binic' (Wp.7 36M).

**Plunging heath approaching Wp.8.**

A woodland climb takes us past a bridleway from **La Ville Morel**, after which we get our first glimpse of the heath-clad escarpments that are so characteristic of this walk. Joining a lane below **La Ville Guyot**, we turn right (Wp.8 49M), sticking with the GR as it descends to the end of the tarmac to recover the coastal path.

After joining a track that briefly touches on the road beside **La Ville Rouault**, we bear right at the 'Barillette' orientation menhir (Wp.9 60M).

**A hidden creek seen at Wp.9**

We then contour round the headland before a steep descent brings us down to the picturesque bay of **Petit Le Havre**, where we cross the

**Petit le Havre**

access road to recover the path (Wp.10 80M). After the next headland, a slightly serpentine climb (intermittently descending as well as weaving from side to side) leads to a major Y-junction just below a picnic table and the end of a dirt track, where we join the 'Vau Madec sentier de decouverte', which is signposted behind the hedge (Wp.11 98M).

**The final descent**

We continue along the coast, turning right at a clearly waymarked junction (Wp.12 108M) to descend along the rocky spur of **Pointe de Bréhin** into the valley of **La Vau Madec**, where we turn left (Wp.13 114M).

When the waymarked itinerary climbs to the left, we stay on the broad trail in the bed of this delightful valley (Wp.14 119M), then fork left at the next two junctions (Wp.15 123M & Wp.16 127M) before climbing to rejoin the waymarked route at a well stabilized dirt track (Wp.17 129M). Turning right, we cross the track accessing Wp.11 at a staggered crossroads (Wp.18 133M). Resuming our southeasterly direction, we follow a minor track that eventually becomes a residential lane, 150 metres from **Rue Duguay Trouin**, 300 from **La Croix Guingard**.

The **Baie de Saint Brieuc** is less celebrated than that of **Mont St. Michel** (see Walk 35), but the sharper escarpment of its shoreline affords better walking, while the bay itself is no less spectacular and barely less dangerous. Happily, there's no risk involved in this fine walk touring the **Presqu'île de Hillion**, which features a lovely little estuary, spectacular rolling coastline, and a striking view on the great grey smudge of mussel beds lining the low water mark.

Bear in mind though, even if the bay is not as notorious as that of **Mont St. Michel**, the tide channels are still treacherous, added to which there's the risk (admittedly very slight, but advertised nonetheless) of the flood gates being opened on the **Pont Rolland** hydroelectric dam. Aimlessly strolling out onto the sands is not recommended, even in fine weather.

* The *traiteur* just after the Mairie at the start of the walk has an excellent range of freshly prepared salads if you want a slightly superior picnic, otherwise the **Bistro à Moules** at Wp.1 offers a variety of tempting looking menus.

**Access:** on foot from **Hillion**.

Hillion church

Parking between the war memorial and the library behind **Hillion** church (Wp.1 0M), we leave the **Place d'Eglise** via the 'Credit Agricole' corner, heading toward the 'Mairie', then take 'Rue de la Tour de Fa', signposted 'Coetmieux/Pont Neuf'. At the roundabout 150 metres later, we continue for 'Coetmieux' on 'Rue de Licantois' (Wp.2 5M).

We follow this road, which is wide but not busy, for a little over a kilometre, passing the 'Lermeleu' access lane, then turning left 75 metres later on a dirt

---

** Wp.8 can also be reached by carrying straight on along the superficially more attractive bridleway through the woods. However, since this is almost permanently muddy, the VTT route is recommended.

track waymarked with 'VTT' (mountain bike) plaques (Wp.3 21M).

Sticking with the 'VTT22' itinerary, we turn right at the first junction of tracks (Wp.4 24M), cross the road at 'La Ville Indeloup' (Wp.5 32M) then turn left 300 metres later (Wp.6 43M)** to join the D34 at the 'Mouette Rieuse' gîte (Wp.7 50M). Turning right, we follow the road as it descends to cross a rivulet, after which there are two ways down to the River Gouessant, the first unmarked but more direct and used by locals, the second an official, slightly more roundabout path. The second has clearly been designed as an alternative to the first, but since both involve crossing a single-wire electric fence, I suggest taking the first unless there's some immediate and manifest reason (a bull might suffice) for avoiding it.

### The pond-like reservoirs

Option 1: 25 metres after the 'La Grandville/50km' speed limit sign (Wp.8 52M), we turn left to cross an electric fence with an insulated hook handle and follow tractor tracks down through a meadow to pass to the right of two large pond-like reservoirs.

Option 2: 50 metres further up the road, just short of the turn-off to 'Tanio' and opposite a 'Louis Guilloux' waypost, a faint way enters the woods above the reservoirs (NE). After running along the top side of the wood, the path drops down to cross an electric fence (no handle!) and join Option 1 at the second reservoir, 150 metres from the road.

Either way, we cross the earth dam at the lower end of the second reservoir, then turn right to descend to the **Gouessant**, where we

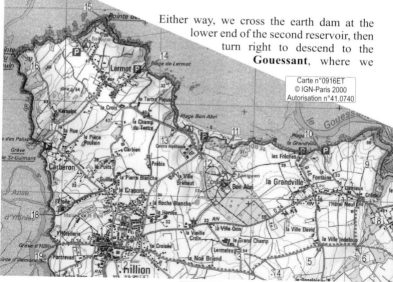

Carte n°0916ET
© IGN-Paris 2000
Autorisation n°41.0740

join the **GR34** (Wp.9 58M). We turn left here and follow the GR along the coast all the way back to **Hillion**, so it's books in packs and eyes on the horizon. After a brief but steep climb across a bluff above a bend in the river, an equally steep descent brings us back to the riverbank and woodland spangled with orchids. As the estuary opens out, the **Chapelle Saint Maurice** comes into view across the sands, and the path dips up and down, snaking its way into the **Baie de Saint Brieuc**, the horizon at low tide striated with row upon row of mussel posts.

We cross two roads accessing **Plage de la Grandville** (Wp.10 83M the first road) then descend behind **Plage de Bon Abris**, ignoring a turning on the right into the dunes (Wp.11 101M). Carrying straight on along the GR, we pass behind a small lagoon into an orchid-filled glade shortly before reaching the **Plage de Bon Abris** road. 75 metres inland, we take the 'Pointe de Guette' lane (Wp.12 108M) climbing past the mussel packing warehouses until a signposted turning on the right takes us back onto the coastal path (Wp.13 112M).

After a tiny detour up the **Plage de Lermot** road, we double back on the right into the car-park (Wp.14 118M) for the final approach to the **Pointe de Guette**, directly behind which, we turn right at a T-junction (Wp.15 131M).

**St. Guimont** *lavoir*

The path then curves in toward **Saint Brieuc** itself, crossing the roof of the **Pointe de Grouin** *blockhaus* (Wp.16 148M) before descending to the **Grève de St Guimont** and its well preserved *lavoir* (Wp.17 164M).

We then pass the signposted turning up to the 'Maison de la Baie' (Wp.18 176M) and continue along the GR until it descends to **Plage de l'Hotellerie** (Wp.19 181M), at which point we turn left and follow the lane back up to the village.

# 24 ERQUY: IN THE FOOTSTEPS OF ASTERIX

**Erquy** is often identified as the village under the magnifying glass on the map at the start of the Asterix books, but its local fame is premised on a far more tangible resource, its fabulous cape, which is embroidered with some of the best beaches in Brittany. An extremely satisfying walk that could be strung out almost indefinitely if you let yourself be tempted by all the natural stopping points en route.

If the weather's fine, don't forget to take your swimming gear. There's a very slight risk of vertigo on the quarry path at the end, which can be avoided by carrying straight on for 'Lac Bleu' at Wp.26.

|  |  |  |
|---|---|---|
| **Strolls** The individual beaches and headlands can easily be reached by road using the Tourist Information Office map. | | **Short Version** Head inland at Wp.20 for 'Lac Bleu' cutting the **Pointe de 4 Vents** headland. |

*in Erquy

**Access:** on foot from **Erquy** (accessible via the **St.Brieuc-Frehel** bus, line 2)

From **Place de l'Eglise** in **Erquy** (Wp.1 0M), we follow 'Rue Notre Dame' up to a Y-junction within sight of a calvary, at which point we fork left along 'Rue de l'Horizon Bleu' (Wp.2 3M). When the road bears right at the junction with 'Allée de l'Horizon Bleu' (Wp.3 8M), we carry straight on along a broad path marked with 'Tour du Cap Erquy' stickers. Maintaining an easterly direction when the path debouches onto 'Chemin de la Louve' and again at the crossroads at the end of **Chemin de la Louve** (Wp.4 15M), we continue on a well stabilized dirt track.

Ignoring all junctions, we follow this track until it crosses a busy local road at 'La Ville es Renais' (Wp.5 31M), 50 metres after which, we fork left (Wp.6). After a signposted junction with the 'Circuit de l'Ilot St. Michel' (Wp.7 36M), our track descends past the meticulously landscaped scar of an old tip and enters mixed woodland.

Sables d'Or at Wp.9

Toward the bottom of the wood, we join the **GR34** at an intersection of paths (Wp.8 43M) where we turn left as indicated by yellow waymarks

Our trail broadens into a stony track that subsequently becomes a lane leading to a waymarked T-junction (Wp.9 48M). The GR turns left here and follows the road round to **Champ du Port**, but so long as the tide is not exceptionally high, it's far more attractive to carry straight on, following an unmarked but well beaten way through the dunes to the sandflats.

Shadowing the curve of the shore and staying well to the left of the main tide channels, we rejoin the GR via the hard behind the **Champ du Port** car-park (Wp.10 69M). Crossing the car-park, we recover the coastal path proper in front of **Ilot Saint Michel**, with its tiny but spectacular chapel.

Carte n°0916ET
© IGN-Paris 2000
Autorisation n°41.0740

We now follow the GR all the way back to **Erquy**, so unless walking and reading at the same time is your thing, stow the book and just enjoy the extraordinary selection of beaches that ensues. The way is obvious and well-waymarked throughout apart from one brief section after Wp.26.

Ilot St. Michel

For the purposes of pacing progress, the GR crosses the **Plage Ilot Saint Michel** car-park (Wp.11 81M) and tunnels through shrubbery before running into 'Rue de la Fosse Eyrand' (Wp.12 88M).

After passing in front of the **Roz Armor** holiday complex, we climb across a low headland then descend to 'Allée de Penthièvre' behind **Plage Le Guen** (Wp.13 101M).

When the road curves inland behind the car-park (Wp.14 107M), we turn right to cross a wooden footbridge and follow a narrow path through deep, dense ferns to reach another road at the western end of **Plage Le Guen** (Wp.15 114M). We turn left here, then right at the lay-by 75 metres later (Wp.16) to recover the coastal path, on which we immediately fork right.

At the next junction, we turn right (Wp.17 125M), descending behind **Plage du Portuais** to the first of the engraved slabs of granite that function as wayposts in the nature reserve.

We follow the 'Pointe de 4 Vents' path up to the 'Aire de Falaise de Portuais' car-park (Wp.18 132M), where we turn right, twice within ten metres.

The granite waypost at Wp.18

The GR snakes round the rim of the cape, then rejoins the main trail cutting across the headland, after which two more 'Pointe de 4 Vents' slabs (Wp.19 147M & Wp.20 151M) indicate our path behind **Plage de Lourtuais**.

Plages de Guen & Lourtuais

We descend almost onto the beach itself before boardwalks take us onto a broad trail heading inland to another '4 Vents' right hand turn (Wp.21 159M). Finally, after crossing the **Vallon de Pissot**, we turn right at a T-junction (Wp.22 170M) to reach the **Pointe de 4 Vents**, and very likely too except on the calmest of days (Wp.23 176M).

The path now curves into the **Baie de St. Brieuc** to the 'Aire de Pointe d'Erquy' car-park (Wp.24 187M). We follow the road for 250 metres then, just short of the old customs cabin on the horizon, turn right on a GR waymarked path (Wp.25 192M).

At the next wayposted junction, we turn right for the *'Four a boules'* (an old furnace formerly used for making cannonballs) (Wp.26 195M). Descending to the left on the nearside of the furnace, we follow a rough corniche path below abandoned quarries until we come to a *'Passage interdite. Danger'* sign (Wp.27 206M), where a rough way climbs to the left to rejoin the main 'Lac Bleu' path (Wp.28 208M). Turning right, we follow the path as it winds alongside then joins the main **Pointe d'Erquy** road (Wp.29 214M).

The **Lac Bleu**, actually a rather murky quarry pond, lies 150 metres down the track to the right, but we stay on the GR, which follows the road for 400 metres to house Nº9 'bis' (Wp.30 221M), where a narrow alley descends on the right to the 'Impasse du Roc'. 200 metres down 'Rue de Tu Es Roc', we again turn right on a waymarked stairway (Wp.31 225M ) descending to the seafront esplanade, which we follow round **Plage du Bourg** before turning left behind a row of flagpoles and taking 'Rue de la Saline' back to the start.

# 25 CAP FRÉHEL & FORT LA LATTE: CLIFFS, HEATH & KIRK DOUGLAS

One of the most famous beauty spots in Brittany, the headland of **Cap Fréhel** is a glorious admix of grand sea views, rugged cliffs, great beaches, and wildly variegated heath. This itinerary takes in all its outstanding features except for the beaches (best further south toward **Sables d'Or**), adding for good measure the evocative fourteenth century **Fort La Latte**.

So where does Kirk Douglas come into all this? Well, **Fort La Latte** is so very evocative it's attracted plenty of moviemakers as well as tourists and featured in the 1958 swashbuckler The Vikings, a film now best known for Tony Curtis' rare 'Viking' wristwatch and a white van trundling along the cliffs behind a bloody 'Viking' sea battle! The incongruities persist. The day we recorded this walk, the only boats in the bay were a couple of eighteenth century corsair sloops. The hinterland stretch of our itinerary is clearly and unequivocally waymarked (except at Wps.6 & 20) with yellow dashes. The coastal stretch is even more obvious! After a preliminary read through, the book can be safely stowed for the best part of the walk.

**Access:** by car

---

**Strolls**

As a glance at the map will indicate, the coastal path can easily be accessed from the principal roads, notably at Wps. 1/12/14/15/16/17, any one of which would be an ideal spot for just stretching your legs and drinking in the views.

---

Our itinerary starts from the **Fort La Latte** car park at the end of the D16a, which is clearly signposted from all the main **Cap Fréhel** approach roads. From the southern entrance of the car-park (Wp.1 0M), we stroll back up the D16a past the **Bellevue Hotel**, then turn right 50 metres after the hotel, as indicated by a waypost and waymarks (Wp.2 3M). After following a minor lane through the hamlet of **La Latte**, we cross the D16 (Wp.3 8M) and continue on tarmac for another 75 metres, then head south on a dirt track until we come a T-junction with another lane (Wp.4 18M).

Turning right, then right again at the next junction 125 metres later (Wp.5), we follow the lane up to the hamlet of **Ville Menier** (Wp.6 25M). Ignoring the new waymarks, which apparently indicate a left hand turn, we maintain direction (NW) on the dirt track passing between the houses.

Reaching a wayposted junction just short of the D16, we double back to the left (Wp.7 30M) then bear right at the oblique Y-junction 50 metres later (Wp.8). Ignoring two minor branch tracks and one major (Wp.9 36M), we continue in a southwesterly direction until our track runs into asphalt and joins the D16 (Wp.10 42M). Turning left, we follow this very modest 'main' road (passing the 'La Ribote' *brasserie-restaurant*) until it swings sharp left, at which point we bear right then immediately turn right (Wp.11 44M) to take a strikingly straight track slicing across the heath.

**Great beaches as seen from the coastal path**

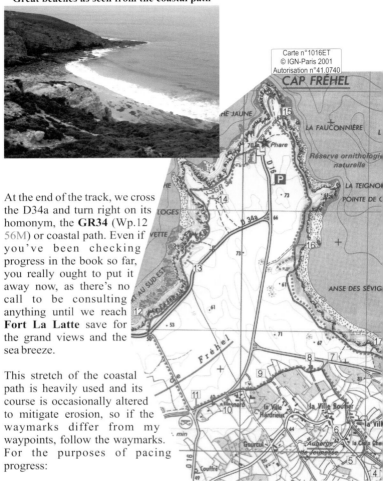

Carte n°1016ET
© IGN-Paris 2001
Autorisation n°41.0740

At the end of the track, we cross the D34a and turn right on its homonym, the **GR34** (Wp.12 56M) or coastal path. Even if you've been checking progress in the book so far, you really ought to put it away now, as there's no call to be consulting anything until we reach **Fort La Latte** save for the grand views and the sea breeze.

This stretch of the coastal path is heavily used and its course is occasionally altered to mitigate erosion, so if the waymarks differ from my waypoints, follow the waymarks. For the purposes of pacing progress:

- At a stubby waypost we fork left, away from the road (Wp.13 66M).

- Just below a small ruin, we pass a crossroads behind **Pointe du Jas**, an optional diversion to the left (Wp.14 77M).

**Rugged cliffs near Wp.14**

- After skirting the lighthouse and its rather unlovely car-park, another option leads to **Cap Fréhel** itself, otherwise we bear right to pass behind the restaurant/souvenir shop, bringing **Fort La Latte** into view (Wp.15 93M).

- The GR briefly broadens to a track as we leave the 'Site Classé de Cap Fréhel' and crosses the end of another track (Wp.16 111M).

- We pass a signposted path accessing the D16 and enter the **Parc de la Latte** (Wp.17 137M).

When the coastal path crosses the main trail between **Fort la Latte** and the car-park, we have a choice of routes (Wp.18 160M).

**Fort La Latte**

We can either simply turn right and follow the crowds back to the car-park or, recommended, carry straight on for 'Saint Geran', staying on the coastal path.

The coastal path divides briefly at an unmarked Y-junction amid a stand of pine 500 metres later (Wp.19 167M). 300 metres after that, when the dense evergreen oak give way to chestnut at 'SOS' post '51' (Wp.20 174M), we take the narrow, unmarked path climbing to the right to return to the car-park.

Carte n°1016ET
© IGN-Paris 2001
Autorisation n°41.0740

# 26 ST. JACUT-DE-LA-MER: WALKING ON WATER

If you happen to be idly flicking through the book and find yourself arrested by the map image, no, it's not wrong, nor are you required to perform some Galilean miracle. The trick is in the timing as this is our most extreme low water walk, in this instance along the sands round the **Presqu'île de St. Jacut**. It's a fine outing with constantly shifting perspectives and features the ruin of a fourteenth century castle, some lovely woodland, numerous beaches, an unusually ornate Martello tower, and an extraordinary array of shells, variously embedded in the budding rock and scattered about the sand like confetti, the latter traditionally collected for decorating graves at All Souls.

You should set off about three hours before low tide and be at the southern end of the **Île des Hébihens** for the return to the mainland <u>no later</u> than an hour after low tide. Tide tables are available at Tourist Information Centres, newsagents and on http://tide.frbateaux.net.

The bay is not notoriously dangerous and you will see plenty of locals out in the middle of nowhere happily grubbing away in the mudflats, not to mention the ostreiculturists casually tooling about the sands apparently intent on driving to Portsmouth. Still, don't venture too far from the shore unless accompanied by someone who knows what they're doing.

* Out of season there's nothing open en route, but there are two recommended eateries nearby, one on the strength of scent and popularity, the other from experience. At the western end of the **Port de Guildo** bridge is the **Restaurant Gilles de Bretagne**, which smells great but was full when we tried to get a table. If the same unhappy fate befalls you, **Les 4 Vents** further up the road at **Notre Dame de Guildo** is a straightforward bistro with good food and some fine local beers.

**Access:** by car or bus

| **Short Version** | **Strolls** |
|---|---|
| The main loop starting at Wp.6. | (a) to Wp.4 and back<br>(b) **Île des Hébihens** from the car-park at **Pointe du Chevet** (see Wp.13) |

To reach the start, from the eastern end of the **Port de Guildo** bridge on the D786 (Bus 14 **St.Malo-St. Cast**), take the narrow lane to the right of the **Hotel/Restaurant de Vieux Chateau**. The walk starts from the **Chateau de Gilles de Bretagne** car-park on the left 300 metres later.

From the car-park (Wp.1 0M), we set off on the **GR34** on a broad trail above the banks of the **Arguenon** estuary, immediately passing behind the spectacular ruins of the castle and descending to the remains of a *lavoir*. The path curves round to a major, waymarked Y-junction (Wp.2 6M), where we fork left, climbing into a long field, at the first corner of which the GR traces an entirely superfluous but pleasant loop through the woods above the estuary before returning to the field a few metres further on. 50 metres later, we take to the water, leaving the GR and forking left to descend to the first of the headland's eleven beaches (Wp.3 14M).

At the end of the next, long beach, **Plage de Vauver**, from where we can already see the church of **St. Jacut**, we rejoin the GR (Wp.4 26M) to cross a low, wooded headland leading to **Plage du Ruet** and a turning circle at the end of a sandy track (Wp.5 37M).

Once again, we leave the waymarked route and wind through the rocks on the beach before climbing the second public stairway to join the D62 (Wp.6 42M).

We continue up the road into the village then double back to the right at the junction with the D26 in front of 'Le Buveur de Lune' (the Moondrinker) *bar/crêperie* (Wp.7 43M).

After following the D26 to the south for 200 metres through the **Hameau des Grandes Marées** (High Tide Hamlet - you'll see why when you cross the dike on the eastern side of the *presqu'île*), we turn left (Wp.8 45M) toward a tall, red-capped water tower on the far side of the bay.

A track between two new houses leads to an open meadow, on the far side of which we climb onto the dike below the municipal campsite and bear left (Wp.9 49M). At the end of the dike, we follow the thin line of picket spiked dunes behind **Plage de la Manchette** then, just west of the main entrance to the campsite, take 'Chemin de la Pissotte' (Wp.10 57M).

**Plage de la Pissotte**

In front of house N°8 (Wp.11 60M), steps lead down to **Plage de la Pissotte**, where we again take to the water, cutting directly across the harbour to the tip of the **Port du Châtelet** quay (Wp.12 64M).

(N.B. this point can be reached directly from **Plage de la Manchette**, but it's muddy and malodorous).

From here you can dispense with the book, as we simply do the tour of the *presqu'île* and the **Île des Hébihens** before rejoining the mainland shortly before Wp.6.

For the purposes of pacing progress, we traverse the sands and a brief band of

**Port du Châtelet (near Wp.12)**

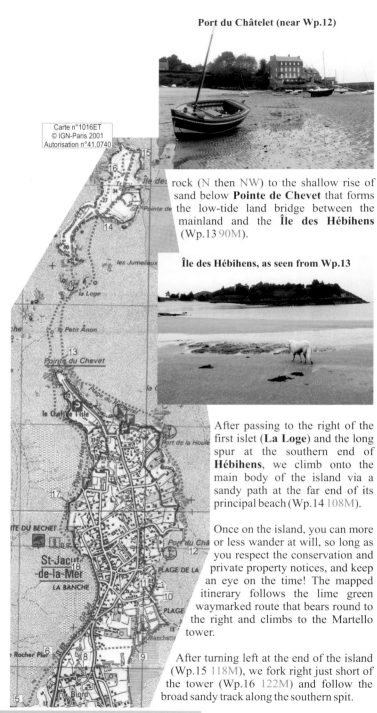

rock (N then NW) to the shallow rise of sand below **Pointe de Chevet** that forms the low-tide land bridge between the mainland and the **Île des Hébihens** (Wp.13 90M).

**Île des Hébihens, as seen from Wp.13**

After passing to the right of the first islet (**La Loge**) and the long spur at the southern end of **Hébihens**, we climb onto the main body of the island via a sandy path at the far end of its principal beach (Wp.14 108M).

Once on the island, you can more or less wander at will, so long as you respect the conservation and private property notices, and keep an eye on the time! The mapped itinerary follows the lime green waymarked route that bears round to the right and climbs to the Martello tower.

After turning left at the end of the island (Wp.15 118M), we fork right just short of the tower (Wp.16 122M) and follow the broad sandy track along the southern spit.

Carte n°1016ET
© IGN-Paris 2001
Autorisation n°41.0740

Once back on the land bridge, we stay on the high ground to return to **Pointe de Chevet**, then cross the weed capped rise on its right hand side (150M) and follow the drier sands along the western shoreline to the southern end of **Plage des Haas** (Wp.17 165M).

Hébihens, near Wp.15

We remain 'underwater' until we reach **La Banche**, the long, muddy bay backed by a boulder embankment below the centre of the village, at which point I recommend climbing up the jetty (Wp.18 169M) and following the esplanade round the curve of the bay. At the southern end of the bay, the sea wall narrows (slightly vertiginously) before rejoining our outward route at Wp.6 (181M). To end the walk, we stay with the waymarked path after Wp.4.

Despite having many traditions in common, one foundation myth Brittany doesn't share with Britain is the Robin Hood legend, though the figure of Maid Marian was imported from the French pastoral tradition and May games. But if ever the old outlaw was in need of a refuge, he'd feel right at home on this gloriously shady walk through fine woodland alongside one of Brittany's most famous salmon spawning streams. A delight from beginning to end.

**Access:** on foot from **Belle Isle en Terre**.

Our itinerary starts behind the new church in **Belle Isle** near the 'Shopi' supermarket, where there's a footbridge and a **GR34a** sign (Wp.1 0M). We follow the municipal access road round to the left toward the football pitch and a large blue gym, then take a grassy track to the right of the gym (Wp.2 3M).

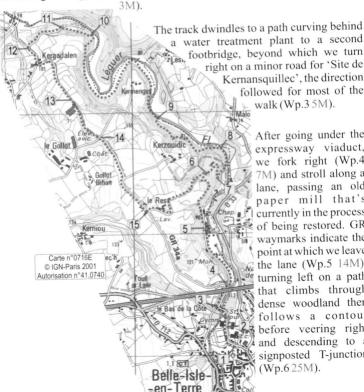

The track dwindles to a path curving behind a water treatment plant to a second footbridge, beyond which we turn right on a minor road for 'Site de Kernansquillec', the direction followed for most of the walk (Wp.3 5M).

After going under the expressway viaduct, we fork right (Wp.4 7M) and stroll along a lane, passing an old paper mill that's currently in the process of being restored. GR waymarks indicate the point at which we leave the lane (Wp.5 14M), turning left on a path that climbs through dense woodland then follows a contour before veering right and descending to a signposted T-junction (Wp.6 25M).

Bearing right, we descend to another waymarked turning on the left (Wp.7 32M) leading to a junction of waymarked paths (Wp.8 37M).

**Robin Hood wood near Wp.9**

Ignoring the yellow waymarked path to the right, we climb to the left along the GR. The path dips up and down below towering beech, describing some extraordinary meanders, including some fairly stiff climbs, then drops down below private land to the riverbank, where we pass the first of several cog-like numbered signposts (Wp.9 40M).

**River & pasture between Wps. 9&10**

Our itinerary then skirts a fenced pasture and goes through four stiles on the outside of a pronounced meander before passing a steep, stepped turning on our left, 100 metres short of the site of an old dam.

After visiting the site of the dam, we take a gentler path (Wp.10 65M) doubling back on the left to merge with the steep stepped turning. We then climb across a rise before descending back to the dam access road in front of a cottage (Wp.11 70M).

**The river below the former dam**

Bearing left, we follow the lane up to a broader road and the **Site de Kernansquillec** car-park (Wp.12 75M). Turning left then left again 100 metres later, we join a dirt track climbing past a junction below farm buildings (Wp.13 84M). Maintaining direction (SE) past the farm buildings, we continue on a country lane, carrying straight on 300 metres later at the 'Kermenguy' junction (Wp.14 89M). 700 metres after that, at the southern end of the **La Rest** hamlet (Wp.15 98M), we turn left, still signposted 'Site de Kernansquillec', then immediately right to follow a dirt track, contouring round the outlying farmsteads of the hamlet before descending into the woods to rejoin our outward route at Wp.6 (108M).

# 28 SAINT NICODÈME: LANDES DE LOCARN & GORGES DU CORONG

This itinerary maybe brief, the walk maybe waymarked, but it amply merits inclusion as it's one of the most beautifully varied circuits in Brittany - <u>not a walk you'd want to miss, under any circumstances</u>. After traversing lovely protected heathland, home to Hen Harrier and Montagu's Harrier, we plunge into fine woodland (beech, birch, ash, oak) to discover the gorge and it's chaos, which is almost as spectacular as **Huelgoat**'s but benefits enormously from being far less well known and far less accessible.

The route is clearly waymarked with the blue silhouette of the harriers for which the area is a designated protection zone and, once you're on the spot, can be followed without consulting the book.

2 | 1¼ H | 4.75 km* | 75m / 75m | ↻ | 0

(* officially 8km)

**Access:** by car

Carte n°0717E
© IGN-Paris 1985
Autorisation n°41.0740

Our itinerary stars 2.3 kilometres west of **Saint Nicodème** on the D20 (dir. 'Locarn') at the 'Aire de Quelenec' carpark, also signposted 'Menhir Paotr Saout' 'Landes de Locarn'. From the carpark (Wp.1 0M), we head southwest, initially alongside then parallel to the road, which we cross after 450 metres to enter the 'Landes de Locarn' (Wp.2 7M).

**The menhir**

Following a broad trail, we traverse lovely heathland and a small stand of oak sheltering an attractive little menhir, then climb a small rise, bringing into view the distant outline of both the **Monts d'Arées** and the **Montagnes Noires**.

A long gentle descent brings us down to the boundary between the heath and farmland, where we reach the end of a dirt track and turn right for 'Gorges du Corong' (Wp.3 29M).

After a gentle stroll along an attractive bracken-lined path, we enter denser woodland and fork right (Wp.4 32M) to stay on the main trail, forking left 75 metres later (Wp.5).

Descending steadily toward the chaos of massive boulders at the heart of the gorge, we ignore a faint path dropping down to the left and continue on the main trail, which leads to the easiest rock-hopping crossing of the chaos.

... an ancient trail ...

On the far bank of the gorge, we turn right on an ancient trail climbing amid lovely woodland interleaved with phantasmagoric rocks (Wp.6 38M).

**Chaos of massive boulders**

The trail soon levels out, winding through the woods alongside the watercourse, splitting briefly amid less dense woods (Wp.7 47M), a couple of hundred metres short of another car-park and the end of a surfaced road. 75 metres up the road, immediately after a small ruin with a well, we turn right for 'Le Quelenec par Les Landes' (Wp.8 53M). After crossing the main watercourse via a dyke, we re-emerge on the heath for a straightforward stroll back to our starting point.

A quarter of this walk is on tarmac, but it's worth it, because between times we have some lovely sunken paths, and our itinerary climaxes with the spectacular **Chaos de Toul Goulic**. Compared to the cataracts of rock at **Huelgoat** and **Corong** (see Walks 15 and 28), the **Chaos de Toul Goulic** is merely a little muddled, but it more than compensates for its lack of in-yer-face rockiness by its seclusion. Submerged in tangled woodland so dense the sky barely gets a look in, it's a wonderfully isolated spot, blessed with a jungle-like fecundity that lends the excursion a real sense of adventure.

If you really can't abide road walking, the short version features the best bits of the full itinerary and no tarmac. The route is meant to be wayposted and waymarked, but at the time of writing, the way and sign posts are either incoherent, or uninformative, or disintegrating, or disappeared, while a long stretch of the local GR seems to have been mislaid, so I'm afraid the book has to be kept handy. Mud is virtually guaranteed, so come well-shod.

### Short Version

**Access:** on foot from **Tremargat**

If you just want to do the loop round the Chaos, park at Wp.16 (2.4km from the D8 between **Guingamp** & **Rostrenen**) and follow the described itinerary to Wp.26 then fork right, returning to Wp.16 500 metres later. There's room for two cars to park at Wp.16 beside the sign indicating that there's a picnic area 500 metres later. If there's no room to park safely here, continue to the picnic area then turn right and descend to Wp.14, where there's ample parking.

From the church square in **Tremargat** (Wp.1 0M), we take the lane starting beside the 'Tremargad Café' for 'Les Druides' campsite, then turn left 575 metres later, still following the signs for the campsite (Wp.2 7M). We follow this lane through pleasant, peaceful, lightly wooded countryside all the way to the hamlet of **Gwernavalou**, where we turn right for 'Toul ar Hotten' (Wp.3 25M). When the main lane swings left, we carry straight on along a roughly surfaced track (Wp.4 32M) then fork right 100 metres later (Wp.5) on an attractive path tunneling through a band of woodland.

This lovely, but intermittently muddy path eventually runs into a dirt track (Wp.6 45M), on which we maintain a northerly direction until we reach the farm of **Le Goaffre**, where we turn left on a grassy track beside a ramshackle barn (Wp.7 52M). The track dwindles to a trail as it passes the entrance to a field then fords a couple of streams before climbing gently to join the end of another dirt track (Wp.8 62M). We follow this track up to the **Keranquere** farmhouse and a T-junction of lanes, where we turn right then immediately left (Wp.9 70M), to continue on dirt track.

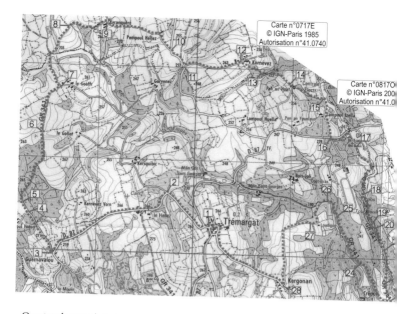

Our track runs into tarmac as we pass another small farmhouse, after which we bear right at a T-junction on the bend of a lane (Wp.10 80M). 150 metres later, we turn left on the lane (not the track just before it) leading to **Kernevez** (Wp.11).

When the lane veers left toward the main farmhouse, we bear right on a dirt track marked with a bridleway plaque (Wp.12 90M). The track soon dwindles to a path descending through predominantly oak woodland to a junction with another path (Wp.13 94M), where we carry straight on, fording a rivulet before climbing to a track just below the 'Pen ar C'hoat Base de Loisirs' camping area (Wp.14 99M).

100 metres to the left, there are a couple of picnic tables and benches beside the lake, which makes a nice spot for a break, otherwise, turn right then immediately left to recover the bridleway on the western side of the camping area. When the bridleway emerges on the dam access road, we turn right (Wp.15 106M) and climb past the largely invisible but rather lovely manor house of **Lampoul Izella** to the D20 and the lane to 'Coat Braz'. We ignore the path descending to the right and, just where the mouth of the **Coat Braz** lane narrows, turn left (Wp.16 110M) on a tiny path descending alongside the road.

At the bottom of the valley, the path swings right then meanders through the woodland alongside the **River Blavet**, dividing briefly (Wp.17 115M) before descending to the banks of the **Blavet**, at this stage an uninspiring little stream. After crossing a minute rise in more open ground choked with bracken and brambles, we reach an unmarked Y-junction, at which point we leave the main trail (which starts to climb into the woodland here) and fork left on a decidedly unpromising looking path (Wp.18 122M).

**Approaching the chaos**

Unpromising or not, this is where the adventure begins as the path weaves through a wild tangle of woodland, soon reaching the first moss and weed frosted boulders at the head of the chaos, and ancient GR-style waymarks rather haphazardly scattered about the trees.

Ducking under overhanging boughs and clambering over occasional rocks, we continue winding through the woods, soon passing two obscure crossing points leading to the paths accessing the main car-park at the end of the D110 (Wps.19 & 20 132M) (the only point at which you're likely to see anyone else in the Chaos), after which the trail gets even fainter.

**More muddle than chaos**

There's little chance of going wrong though, as the surrounding trees are too entangled to permit much straying off path.

**... a particularly lovely pool ...**

Following common sense and the waymarks, which generally coincide, we shadow the chaos, passing a particularly lovely pool (the largest encountered en route) (Wp.21 141M), then gradually climb away from the watercourse to rejoin the main trail left at Wp.18 (Wp.22 150M).

Bearing left, we stroll along to a T-junction where we turn right (Wp.23 153M) and descend into a lovely wooded valley. Reaching a Y-junction, we carry straight on (the right hand fork) (Wp.24 160M), staying on the left bank of the stream, passing a very minor, unmarked path climbing to the right and, 50 metres later, a broader trail (Wp.25 168M).

Thereafter, we pass a rather rickety looking footbridge and come to a major junction, with waymarking arrows indicating a ford down to our left. We cross the stream via the ford or the footbridge (Wp.26 171M) and follow the main trail as it climbs in a southerly direction to join a dirt track (Wp.27 176M). The track heads SE then S before running into tarmac and coming to a crossroads at the hamlet of **Kergonan** (Wp.28 186M), where we simply turn right and follow the lane back to the start.

**An alarming waypost at Wp.23**

Damming watercourses and drowning a lot of trees is generally thought a pretty despicable act in the present ecological climate, but it can have happy results. The **Lac de Guerlédan** at the heart of Brittany, where 17 locks on the Nantes to Brest canal were submerged, is a case in point - a lovely, long, sinuous reservoir cradled in rolling countryside patched with higgledy-piggledy fields and wild mixed woodland featuring ash, oak, chestnut, birch, beech and fir.

Doubtless it was a lovely, long, sinuous waterway before, but it's hard to believe the original landscape was more beguiling than the man-made lake we see today. Better still, the lake is snared in such a web of hiking and biking and riding trails that it would take weeks to work through all the potential walks in the area.

Given its length, the walk description may look a little intimidating, but in fact it's very easy as on the outward leg we simply follow a disused railway line and the waymarking plaques where it's been breached by new roads, while on the return leg we follow the 'Sentier de Guerlédan' wayposts and the <u>new</u> GR waymarks (slightly different from the version of the **GR341N** that appears on the IGN map) - except at Wp.32.

The 'Sentier de Guerlédan', a 35km tour of the entire lake, is incomplete at present, but is scheduled to be opened shortly after the present publication goes to press. The gap in the projected path that would change our itinerary is between **Beau Rivages** and the **Ecluse de Nicolleau** (also known as **Bellevue**). At the time of writing, there is no sign of a shoreline path for this stretch.

* The walking is easy, the exertion rating a reflection of length alone.

| Access: | Strolls | Short Versions |
|---|---|---|
| by car or bus | There are countless obvious stroll options from the various access points to the railway line and lake. | (a) **Belle Vue** loop - see Wps.5 & 48<br>(b) **Beau Rivages** loop - see Wp.11<br>(c) **Bois de Caurel** loop - see Wps. 20/21 to 26 |

Our itinerary starts at the western end of the lake, just off the N164, in the lay-by car park opposite the entrance to the **Abbaye de Bon Repos** (Wp.1 0M), originally built and named in honour of a local noble who enjoyed an al fresco nap on the spot. We stroll back up to the N164 and, 50 metres to the left, take the minor lane (not the D44) in front of the bus-stop, signposted 'Allées Couverte de Niscuis' (Wp.2), then turn right 100-metres later on the broad, graveled track of the old railway line (Wp.3 5M).

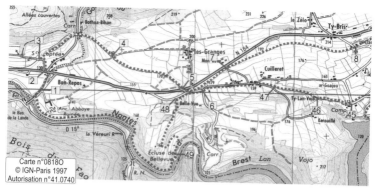

And that's all you really need to know till Wp.18 as, for the next couple of hours, the walk follows the railway line and the blue plaques where it's been breached by development. In the meantime, the text is merely for pacing progress and having an idea of what to expect.

After crossing the **Gorges du Daoulas**, we carry straight on at a crossroads of bridleways (Wp.4 17M). A little over 500 metres later, we re-cross the N164 (Wp.5) and bear left behind a former signals station, as indicated by the blue plaques, briefly following a lane before recovering the railway line (Wp.6 29M). Line and road run alongside one another for a while until we cross a lane (Wp.7 33M), after which they gradually diverge. A second lane is crossed below the hamlet and one time station of **Ti-Bris** (Wp.8 50M), where we carry straight on for 'Caurel', soon crossing a third lane (Wp.9) and a farm track (Wp.10 61M).

The fourth lane (Wp.11 72M), which is preceded by a railway sleeper bench and linesman's cabin, descends to **Beau Rivages**. Those doing Short Version (b) can turn right here or at Wp.12 to descend to Wp.39 or Wp.38. Otherwise, we continue along the railway line, passing a waymarked trail descending to the right 250 metres later (Wp.12). Ignoring a couple of faint yellow crosses, we stick with the railway line as it runs parallel to and then crosses a lane (Wp.13 87M) on the outskirts of **Caurel**.

We cross another lane 150 metres later (Wp.14) and yet another 300 metres after that (Wp.15 96M). The track briefly dwindles to a path as it skirts the village football field then traverses a small bridge (another short version option, the lane below the bridge descends to Wp.21) before crossing a final lane at **Pors Very** (Wp.16 105M).

We carry straight on at a crossroads of tracks (Wp.17 115M) then, 400 metres later, turn right (Wp.18 120M) on a lane descending toward the lake.

After turning right again at the T-junction 100 metres later, signposted 'GR341' and 'Sentier de Guerlédan' (Wp.19), we stay on the tarmac for another 200 metres then fork left (ignoring an old GR cross) to follow the **Sentier de Guerlédan** (Wp.20 125M).

A succession of boardwalks traverse marshy ground to reach a small lakeside carpark, where there's a remarkably clean, eco-friendly public toilet. 40

**Near Wp.20**

metres up the lane accessing the carpark, we turn left on a forestry track leading into the **Bois de Caurel** (Wp.21 137M).

When the track starts to climb 375 metres later, we fork left on a GR-waymarked path (Wp.22 148M).

**The lake, as seen below Wp.21**

We now follow the new GR waymarks all the way back to Wp.6, unless the mapboards indicate that a new path has been opened up between **Beau Rivages** and the **Ecluse de Nicolleau**, in which case that might be preferable as it would, presumably, involve less tarmac.

Our path weaves its away along the shore, constantly dipping up and down, and passing numerous shaley beaches. After traversing a high, heather clad bluff, the path passes behind the double fangs of twin creeks, at the second 'tooth' of which, we bear left, staying alongside the shore and ignoring a faint trail climbing back into the woods (Wp.23 169M).

A second steep climb to the right (Wp.24 175M) takes us onto a platform from where we can see the dam wall. We then pass a small forestry cabin and a spectacular quarry pit before a steep descent takes us back to the water's edge. After following the shoreline to a small mooring beach, we climb back into the woods (Wp.25 182M) to rejoin the track we left earlier (Wp.26 184M). For Short Version (c), turn right here, otherwise we turn left.

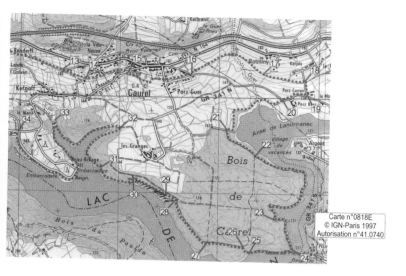

**Approaching Wp.30**

We ignore a branch climbing to the right (Wp.27 189M) then turn left at a T-junction (Wp.28 196M) and continue along the main trail for another 125 metres before bearing left (Wp.29) on a narrower path leading to a long, rugged bluff overlooking the lake and the resort of **Beau Rivage**.

**Beau Rivage** eventually disappears behind a prominent rocky outcrop, just short of which we fork left on an obscurely waymarked path (Wp.30 204M) descending steeply back to the shore. After ignoring a path climbing to the right (Wp.31 211M), we make what seems like an interminable detour into the jester's cap of creeks that precedes **Beau Rivage**. At the head of the more easterly creek (Wp.32 221M), we have a choice of routes.

All the waymarks suggest continuing straight on along the main trail to **Les Granges**, after which the GR uses the D111 to reach **Beau Rivage**. And yet lying down to our left, behind new waymarking crosses, are a couple of perfectly serviceable boardwalks traversing the marshy area at the head of the more easterly creek. The catch is that there are no such boardwalks at the head of the more westerly creek.

However, the un-bridged marshy patch is only a couple of metres long, so unless you're walking after a prolonged period of heavy rain, I reckon it's worth taking the risk of getting your feet wet, rather than trudging all the way up to the road. Anyone with an allergy to wet feet, continue along the waymarked route. Risk-takers turn left with me to cross the boardwalks!

After traversing the narrow watercourse at the head of the western creek (Wp.33 231M), we turn left and follow a well stabilized trail into **Beau Rivage**, which boasts three restaurants and the sort of ambience that will probably have you hurrying back to the woods. The trail leads into a road, which we follow for a kilometre, before turning left (Wp.34 251M) and left again 200 metres later (Wp.35) at the **Lavoir Goaz Vioc'h** into the **Bois de Keriven**.

At first the path loses little altitude, but then it shimmies through a mini-rollercoaster and drops to within twenty metres of the water's edge to a faint junction where we turn right (Wp.36 271M) for a short but stiff climb up to a dirt track (Wp.37 274M). Turning right again, we follow this track into the hamlet of **Keriven**, where we double back to the left (Wp.38 278M) to join a delightful sunken path that descends gently between trees before veering north and broadening to a track running alongside fields.

When the track emerges on a lane (Wp.39 292M), we turn left, then fork left nearly 500 metres later (100 metres after the solitary house) on an unmarked track (Wp.40 299M) leading to the **Kermadec** farm hamlet.

After a brief stretch on tarmac, we carry straight on (Wp.41 305M) along a broad bridleway that contours round a house before dwindling to a path dropping down to the end of a tiny lane (Wp.42 310M). The first stretch of the shoreline path marked on the map here has crumbled away, obliging us to walk up the lane for 175 metres before turning left on a track (Wp.43) that immediately dwindles to a path crossing a ridge of rock before rejoining the shore path for the approach to the fishing stage at **Trégnanton** (Wp.44 321M).

Again, we follow the lane climbing away from the lake, sticking with it until it veers southwest to a roofless ruin, where we fork left on a minor lane signposted 'Sentier Pietonnier Goajo' (Wp.45 330M).

At the end of the lane, we turn left (Wp.46 335M) on a grassy path skirting private property and tunneling through yet more attractive woodland along a lovely sunken alley. When this emerges on a lane, we turn left then immediately right (Wp.47 342M) and maintain a westerly direction at three successive junctions to rejoin our outward route at Wp.6.

Instead of re-crossing the N164, we carry straight on after the signals station, passing the entrance to the **Bellevue** quarry before turning left on a road marked with a bridleway plaque and signposted 'Ecluse Nicolleau' (Wp.48 356M).

**The canal near the end of the walk**

The map shows this road as a nice little track. It ain't. It's been widened and surfaced and is utterly charmless. Even less beguiling is the sight of the quarry as we near the end of the road. But bear with me, because at the end of the road, starting beside the former lock-keeper's cottage, is a lovely tow path (Wp.49 369M) that makes for a delightful end to the walk.

A little over one-and-a-half kilometres later, we pass the spectacular ruins of the abbey and reach the canal bridge, 100 metres away from our starting point.

**The canal bridge**

Elsewhere, we walk *on* the Emerald Coast, but this itinerary could claim the title of the Emerald Walk, traversing as it does some fabulously verdant woodland before visiting the moss mantled boulders of the *chaos* that blocks the upper reaches of the **River Gouët**.

Though never far from the river, this is not strictly speaking a riverside walk, certainly not if you're picturing a nice level tow path, as the greater part of the itinerary is in undulating woodland, with enough dips and rises to make the track profile look like a tachogram. Once on trail, the route is obvious, the need to consult the book negligible.

*I haven't actually been inside the **Couleur Cafe/Restaurant**, but the landlord is friendly, the place looks nice, and it's perfectly located for mid-morning coffee followed by a meal after visiting the Chaos.

**Strolls**
Wps.1-4 & Wps.9-13

**Short Versions**
(a) 'Circuit de Ste. Anne du Houlin'
**Pont Noir** to **Ste. Anne du Houlin**
(b) **Chaos de Gouët** from **Ste. Anne du Houlin** on the D40

**Access:** by car or bus (schooldays only - Line 18 **Saint Donan-Champ de Mars**)

The walk starts from **Ploufragan**'s *'base de loisirs'* car-park on the D45 at the eastern side of **Le Pont Noir** over the **River Gouët** (Wp.1 0M). We cross the bridge onto the left bank of the river, turn left at the junction with the D36, then left again 75 metres later to join the 'Circuit de Ste. Anne du Houlin' bridleway (Wp.2 5M). And that's all you really need to know for the next five kilometres, as we simply follow the waymarked bridleway all the way to the hamlet of **Ste. Anne**.

The trail winds between well-spaced birch, beech, chestnut and oak, and we rapidly put the busy road behind us, as we dip up and down, generally following a balcony path but occasionally approaching the riverbank.

We fork left at a signposted junction (Wp.3 20M) into denser, darker woodland carpeted with ferns and wildflowers, and the peace and quiet deepens, broken only by birdsong and the occasionally sculling of a boat on the river. Carrying straight ahead on the main trail at a crossroads (Wp.4 36M), we skirt a large inlet, bearing left at a signposted junction with a track from 'St. Donan' (Wp.5 46M) and again at a footbridge across a stream beside a water-testing hut (Wp.6 49M).

The dips and rises become more pronounced after the inlet until we reach a waymarked Y-junction (Wp.7 79M), where we fork left to descend to the river. At the river (Wp.8), carry straight on for Short Version A.

Ste. Anne

Otherwise, turn right to reach the D40, **Ste. Anne** and the strategically located **Couleur Cafe/Restaurant**.

To continue into the Chaos, we cross the road bridge and take the signposted path up the right bank of the river (Wp.9 83M), at which point a walk that has been 'merely' lovely becomes idyllic and almost other worldly, both the bird cries and the aspect of the river lending our itinerary a tropical air.

... a tropical air ...

The path passes an old mill race and snakes its way through tangled woodland rimed with a thick frosting of moss.

Climbing away from the river to a T-junction with a mountain bike itinerary (Wp.10 95M), we turn right then immediately right again, briefly intersecting with the mountain bike (**VTT**) route for a second time before descending back to the riverbank.

At a Y-junction amid a tall stand of poplar, we leave the waymarked **GRP** (which we've been following since **Ste. Anne**) and carry straight ahead on the right hand fork (Wp.11 100M). Our path divides briefly at the far end of a pine wood (Wp.12 105M), then traverses a water meadow, after which we pass a wooden footbridge and a second water testing hut before rejoining the **GRP** (Wp.13 112M). 300 metres later, we re-cross the river via a stone footbridge (Wp.14 117M) and turn left toward the **Chaos de Gouët**.

A moderate chaos (between Wps 15&16)

The Chaos is pretty sedate at this stage, but none the less pretty for that, and begins to get a bit more rambunctious after we pass a second wooden footbridge in front of the partially restored ruin of **Le Moulin de St. Meen** (Wp.15 128M). We continue upstream amid clouds of dragon flies until we reach the third wooden footbridge (Wp.16 143M).

Crossing back onto the right bank, we head back downriver, once again on the **GRP**. We stick with the waymarked route as it runs through a natural tunnel

(Wp.17 150M) then, 500 metres later, ignore the signposted **GRP** turning on the right for 'Ste. Anne' (Wp.18 158M) and carry straight on to rejoin our outward route at the stone footbridge (Wp.14 162M), from where we follow the same path back to **Ste. Anne** (193M). The path back to **Pont Noir** begins 50 metres up the road to the right (Wp.19). 300 metres from the road, we briefly join a broader trail but almost immediately fork right (Wp.20 200M) on a narrow path climbing steeply away from the river.

Once again, the route is straightforward and well signposted, though the official distances are inaccurate except for the last one at turning N°4. All the others overestimate the distance. As with the initial stretch on the left bank, there are lots of ups and downs, though happily these diminish toward the end. For the purposes of pacing progress, we pass four paths coming in from the right:

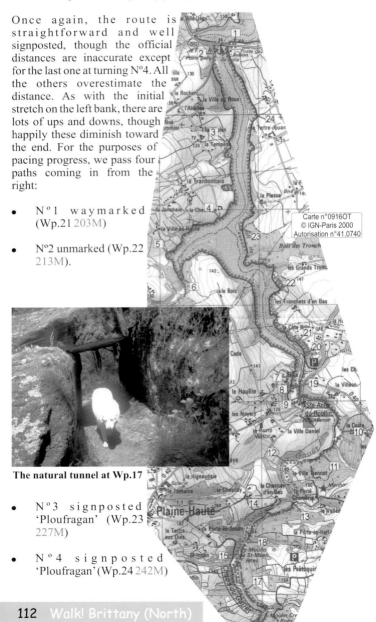

Carte n°0916OT
© IGN-Paris 2000
Autorisation n°41.0740

- N°1 waymarked (Wp.21 203M)

- N°2 unmarked (Wp.22 213M).

**The natural tunnel at Wp.17**

- N°3 signposted 'Ploufragan' (Wp.23 227M)

- N°4 signposted 'Ploufragan' (Wp.24 242M)

As a rule, I avoid describing itineraries that are freely available elsewhere, but in this instance I've made an exception to highlight the excellent work being done by the departmental authorities in **Côtes d'Armor**, signposting and promoting walking and cycling routes throughout the region. The present itinerary is taken from a series of eleven loose-leaf pocket guides that give you the opportunity to explore in detail any given area within the *departement*. In this instance, it's the pastoral and agricultural heartland of **Côtes d'Armor** (there are days when the traffic in the villages is composed mostly of tractors) around the austere but beautifully preserved fortified medieval town of **Moncontour**.

The object of our itinerary is **La Roche au Cerf** (so named because deer regularly came to drink at the ford), a picturesque stepping stone bridge over the **River Lié** that has been in use since the middle ages. The walk is immaculately signposted and the paths are well maintained. There are some access restrictions during the hunting season (October to April), but so long as you're not walking at the weekend, these should not effect the present itinerary. If in doubt, ask at the **Moncontour** tourism office.

**Access:** on foot from **Langast**

| Stroll |
| --- |
| Turn left at Wp.4 to return via Wp.24 |

| Alternative Walks |
| --- |
| See 'Au fil des Côtes d'Armor…balades en Pays de Moncontour' available from the **Moncontour** campsite and the tourism office. |

The walk starts at the **Etang de Fromelin** recreation area on the D22 to the south of **Langast** (Wp.1 0M). We cross the dividing wall between the *etang* and its overflow reservoir and bear left to the signposted start of the itinerary ('Les Essarts, La Roche au Cerf, Les Buttes'), a narrow path descending east between fields. The path soon veers south and crosses a stream to reach a T-junction, where we turn right (Wp.2 6M). We cross the road 100 metres later and briefly follow the course of the stream before bearing left to skirt a fenced meadow.

Ignoring a signposted path on the right for 'Les Buttes' (Wp.3 15M), we climb away from the stream, passing a path doubling back to the left for 'Langast' (Wp.4 18M). Maintaining direction (S), we join the end of a dirt track from **Les Buttes**, along which we turn left (S) on another path for 'La Roche au Cerf' (Wp.5 21M). The path feeds into the end of a second dirt track which we follow past an unmarked turning on the right (Wp.6 27M) until we reach the farming hamlet of **La Ville ès Besnard** (Wp.7 31M).

We turn left on the lane through the village then right 150 metres later (Wp.8) and right again 250 metres after that (Wp.9 37M) on a grassy trail signposted 'Les Essarts'. The trail descends to another signposted junction (Wp.10 42M) where we carry straight on for 'Les Essarts par La Roche au Cerf', turning right 75 metres later at a T-junction with a variant path from 'Plessala'(Wp.11).

After passing a track that forks off to the left (Wp.12 47M) and a bridleway that doubles back to the left (Wp.13 53M), we pass a tiny spring cum shrine and, on the right bank of the river, the **Moulin des Essarts**.

**Stepping stones at Wp.16**

Staying on the left bank, we climb to a lane, where we bear right (Wp.14 67M) then turn right 50 metres later (Wp.15) on a narrow track descending to the **La Roche au Cerf** stepping stones, now sadly superceded by a footbridge (Wp.16 73M).

Having crossed the river, we bear right on a track climbing to the **Cassebreil** farmhouse where we again bear right (Wp.17 78M) to stay on the dirt track as it passes through a spectacular alley of beech. Ignoring a major trail climbing to the left (Wp.18 83M) and subsequent logging tracks branching off to left and right, we follow the main track along a contour before curving round a tennis court to a lane at the much reconstructed **Château des Essarts** (Wp.19 90M).

**Rolling pasture between Wps.18 & 19**

Turning right, we follow the lane between the farm buildings and round to the north. Ignoring a waymarked trail climbing to the left (Wp.20 103M), we bear right at a junction of lanes 150 metres later (Wp.21), then right again after another 150 metres for 'Le Roscoët' (Wp.22 109M).

This lane climbs between farm buildings to reach a junction with a broad track where we have a choice of routes (Wp.23 115M). We can either follow the signposted route on the right for 'Langast', rejoining our outward route at Wp.10, or (as mapped) stay on the lane for another 600 metres, bearing right at the first junction and left at the second, to rejoin our outward route at **La Ville ès Besnard**.

From Wp.7, we return to **Langast** the same way with the option of forking right on the upper path at Wp.4. This path broadens to a fieldside track that crosses the D22 at a lay-by just above the crossing point at the start of the walk.

We double back to the left at a private property notice 150 metres later (Wp.24 149M), rejoining our outward route at Wp.2.

Carte n°0917E
© IGN-Paris 2001
Autorisation n°41.0740

A glance at the map may suggest this itinerary is a large waste of space, as one hardly needs a description for simply circling a lake. In fact, the walk earns it's place in part because it's so hard to find! You could spend hours driving round the tangle of lanes to the north of **Jugon les Lacs** and never know the **Arguenon** was there at all, it's so well hidden amid otherwise rather bland looking countryside. It's more than worth the effort though, as this long narrow reservoir is flanked by some really lovely woodland (beech, birch, oak, ash, chestnut) and a path that at once defies belief (you really had to *want* to make a path here, nature doesn't help at all) and elicits gasps of admiration for the boardwalks and stairways the authorities have installed.

Better still, it's so secluded and, it has to be said, so arduous, you'll probably have the place to yourself apart from the odd local fishermen or a boating enthusiast sculling along the water... given all the ups and downs, you might wish for a boat yourself.

Though never vertiginous, the path is narrow and traverses numerous brief but precipitous slopes, so the walk is not recommended for the unsure of foot or after heavy rain.

| 4 | | 2H | 7.7 km | | 250m / 250m | ↻ | 0 |

**Access:** by car *

* As indicated in the introduction, just chancing upon this walk isn't entirely obvious since the lake is tucked away in apparently seamless countryside. The simplest approach is to take the 'Pledeliac / St. Igneuc' exit from the N176 between **Lamballe** and **Dinan,** and drive into **St. Igneuc**. Set the odometer at 0 as you pass the church and follow the D16, signposted 'Pleven'. Fork right at km1.4 (the second **Jugon les Lacs** mapboard) and follow the 'Lac de l'Arguenon' lane, ignoring all branches, until you reach the **Lorgeril** lay-by at km3.2.

In terms of orientation, finding the start is the hardest part of this walk, as we now simply tour the lake (clockwise) between the **Lorgeril** dam and the **Tournemine** rowing club. From the lay-by (Wp.1 0M), we take the **GRP** for 'Pleven' along the western flank of the lake, and that's all you really need to know, so if time-keeping's not your thing, stow the book, sweat, and enjoy.

The track at the start soon dwindles to a path winding through the woods before climbing the first escarpment and tracing a long dogleg round the head of a creek, where we cross a footbridge and turn right (Wp.2 18M). Shortly afterwards, we ignore an old path climbing to the left (Wp.3 21M) and continue squirming along the shore, crossing a second footbridge, where we again turn right (Wp.4 28M).

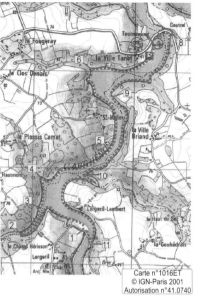

A long, blessedly level stretch passes a couple of trails climbing to the left (Wp.5 43M), after which a 'VTT' (mountain bike) waypost confirms that the going gets easier for a while. Immediately after a fifth footbridge (number three being little more than a line of pallets laid across a muddy watercourse), we fork right at a Y-junction (Wp.6 60M) and the rollercoaster is back for a last little blast of up and down before we emerge in a long, flat field, just short of the **Tournemine** boathouse.

Carte n°1016ET
© IGN-Paris 2001
Autorisation n°41.0740

We turn right on the road behind the boathouse (Wp.7 73M), leaving the **GRP** and crossing onto the eastern flank of the lake to pick up a yellow waymarked path for the return leg (Wp.8 77M).

Rollercoastering resumes, though a long, relatively level stretch does precede the largest stairway on this itinerary (visible from the outward leg), which traverses a prominent outcrop of rock (Wp.9 83M).

**The stairway at Wp.9**

Thereafter, it's up and down again, including a couple of sections with rope handrails. The path then veers away from the shore (Wp.10 102M) and crosses a footbridge over a creek, after which it levels out for a good 500 metres before another rope banister ascent climbs to a boardwalk within sight of the approach road and the track at the start of the itinerary. A steep, stepped, but skittery descent brings us almost back to the water's edge for a final, mini-rollercoaster. The path levels out for the last 200 metres preceding the road, where we turn right (Wp.11 118M) to return to the start.

# 34 CANCALE: A HODGEPODGE OF HEADLANDS

Perhaps the finest bit of coastline in **Ille et Vilaine** and proof positive that tourist friendly place names like 'The Emerald Coast' are not merely the caprice of marketing men, but can be an accurate reflection of what lies on the ground - or, in this instance, in the sea. The outward leg of the walk looks and sounds complex, but is actually quite straightforward and is clearly waymarked with blue dashes. The return along the coast is a dream in green.

The only drawback to this lovely itinerary is that when we did the walk in May there were an inordinate number of vipers basking in the sun beside the coastal path - sometimes there seemed to be one slithering away every ten metres or so. On the assumption that it wasn't a single snake stalking us for a bit of a laugh, I can only presume the population is unusually large hereabouts. They are, of course, more frightened of you than you are of them (really!), but take heed if you're walking with children or dogs. Sticking your snout into the scrub to investigate that interesting rustling (I'm talking about the dogs here), is not a good idea.

| 3 | 3¼ H | 12.4 km | 250m / 250m | ↻ | 3* |

* at **Pointe du Grouin** and **Port Mer**

**Access:** by car or bus

**Stroll**
**Pointe du Grouin**

**Short Version**
Turn right at Wp.7, cutting out the **Pointe du Nid**

The walk starts from the small picnic area/lay-by at the top of 'Rue de Port Pican' just off the D201 north of **Cancale** (the **Port Pican** bus stop on the Cancale-St.Coulomb-St.Malo line) (Wp.1 0M).

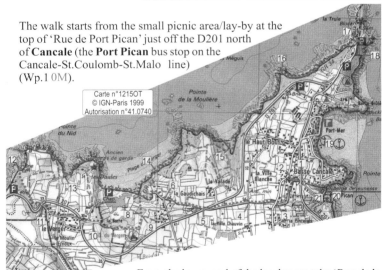

Carte n°1215OT
© IGN-Paris 1999
Autorisation n°41.0740

From the lower end of the lay-by, we take 'Rue de la Basse Cancale' under the D201 and turn left 100 metres later, immediately after house N°22 (Wp.2). Following an attractive trail between the houses, we emerge on 'Impasse de la Hisse', which we follow to a crossroads (Wp.3 7M).

Carrying straight on, we continue along a lane and the dirt track it runs into before returning to tarmac at a junction near a converted mill (Wp.4 11M). Maintaining direction on the ensuing lane (W), we re-cross the D201 450 metres later (Wp.5 17M) and continue into the hamlet of **La Gaudichais**, where we branch right at a house called 'La Corbiere' (Wp.6 24M).

El Verger lagoon, near Wp.5

After 150 metres, the branch lane becomes a dirt track, which we follow down to a junction of waymarked routes behind **Plage du Verger** (Wp.7 28M).

We take the path to the left, turning left again 140 metres later (Wp.8) then right 50 metres after that (Wp.9) to follow a grassy track skirting the **Notre Dame de Verger** campsite.

Near Wp.10

When the track debouches on a narrow lane, we turn left (Wp.10 40M) then almost immediately left again to pass in front of the 'Verger' bus-stop and re-cross the D201 onto 'Rue de Hurlevent'.

Baie de Guisclin, from Wp.12

At the far end of **Rue de Hurlevent**, we cross the D201 once again (Wp.11 49M), joining the **GR34** on a pleasant, hedgerow lined path leading to the true coastal path on **Pointe du Nid** (Wp.12 56M).

There's no call to be reading a walk description here, as we now follow the well-marked GR all along the coast, a pretty obvious passage anyway, so turn right, stow the book, and enjoy.

If you care to measure your progress against mine, we traverse **Pointe du Nid** and descend to a first small beach below **Les Daules** (Wp.13 68M), then climb

The Emerald Coast near Wp.13

over **Pointe de les Daules** before descending to the **Anse de Verger** car-park. A sandy path runs along behind the beach back to Wp.7 (87M), beyond which we continue trudging through the sand until a firmer path climbs away from the eastern end of the beach (Wp.14 93M) to cross **Pointe de la Mouliniere**.

We then descend to a second nameless beach (Wp.15 109M) from the far end of which we climb back onto the uplands. After snaking our way along below the road (taking an obvious but vertiginous shortcut across a three-metre high retaining wall if so inclined), we cross the penultimate headland, bringing into view the signals post on **Pointe du Grouin** (Wp.16 128M).

The second nameless beach

At the track beside the signals building (Wp.17 141M), we can either stroll out to the end of the headland or take an unmarked shortcut down to rejoin the GR as it heads south toward the chateau on **Barbe Brulée**. Forking left at a Y-junction after 150 metres (Wp.18), we contour round a campsite and pass an impressive gun emplacement, then descend to **Port de Mer**.

At the far end of the promenade, we recover a narrow path (signposted 'Le Port') a few metres up the main access road ('Rue Henri Laurent') (Wp.19 170M). A final, infinitely gentle climb leads us onto **Pointe du Chatry** and into **Port Pican**, where we rejoin the blue waymarked route used at the beginning of the walk. Just short of the Youth Hostel (the large building with tongues of the slate roof touching the ground), we fork right (Wp.20 186M) and follow a narrow path up to a T-junction (Wp.21), where we turn left to return to the starting point.

# 35 CHERRUEIX: POLDERS & DIKES, THE BAIE DE MONT ST. MICHEL

The title tells it all, really, as this is precisely what we see - or don't see depending upon how you respond to the terrain, since what individual walkers make of this excursion will vary widely according to taste, temper and personal requirements. For many, the great flat expanse of the **Baie de Mont St. Michel** is an endlessly fascinating waterland, a frontier between elements in which neither water nor land is entirely of itself, a unique eco-system in which man and nature conspire both against and with one another, an eerie, quasi-mystical landscape to be treated with the reverence and deference ordinarily reserved for the world's great deserts. For others, it's just flat.

Personally, I found it at once weird, dispiriting and moving. Whatever your sentiments, the bay itself is not to be explored alone. It's notoriously dangerous with galloping tides herding the ignorant into a labyrinth of quicksand.

If you do want to get out on the sands, take the **Cherrueix** Train Marin (a tractor and trailer 'train' that tours the bay) or a guided walk (www.decouvertebaie.com or www.cheminsdelabaie.com). The present itinerary is a straightforward tour of the dikes and polders on the border, if such a thing can be defined, between the land and the sea. Love it or loathe it, you've probably never done a walk quite like it.

*Le Paddock** in **Cherrueix** in the **Place de l'Eglise** is an excellent little restaurant offering limited but imaginative menus for around 15 euros and special dishes of the day for 10 euros. The asparagus (a local specialty) is particularly good and the knuckle-end of lamb ('souris', yes, that *souris*!), though not coming from the prohibitively expensive 'pre-salted' sheep that graze on the fens, is highly recommended.

**Access:** by car

The walks starts 100 metres east of **Cherrueix** on the track opposite the 'Pichardiere' farm, just short of the solitary western landmark on the walk, the **Chapelle de Ste. Anne** (Jesus' granny, no relation to the duchess, see below). From the line of boulders blocking vehicular access (Wp.1 0M), we stroll along the embankment toward the chapel and the distant Prussian helmet of **Mont St. Michel**.

**The Chapelle de Ste. Anne**

Passing directly behind the chapel, we continue along the dike and that's really all you need to know, as we simply follow the dike for the next five kilometres, hang a right, hang another right a kilometre later and then Anne's-your-aunty, you're back at the beginning. What you make of the interim depends entirely on your own personal engagement with the empty space.

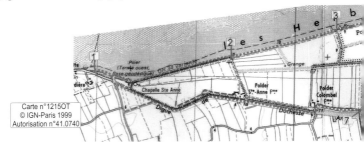

The dike path soon passes a branch to the **Polder Ste. Anne** farm (Wp.2 20M) then goes through a red gate at the next major junction (Wp.3 36M). The small outcrop of rock visible in the distance to the left of **Mont St. Michel** is the **Rocher de Tombelaine**, said to be the burial place of Gargantua's mother, **Gargamelle**, and a symbol of the evil against which St. Michel is battling.

500 metres after the gate, we have to scale a low wooden fence (take note if you've got a heavy dog), after which two tracks cross polders to our right (Wp.4 60M & Wp.5 73M).
We take the second of these tracks, signposted 'Digue de la Duchesse Anne', the dike taking its name from the Breton duchess whose marriage to Charles VIII brought Brittany into France.

**Polder, between Wps. 5&6**

Following the broad metalled track inland, we cross a series of intermediary dikes, at the second of which the **GR34** branches off to the left, while we continue inland, maintaining direction on the lane past the **Mauny** farm.

Just before the next farm, we turn right on the tree lined (poplar then cherry), yellow-waymarked **Digue de la Duchesse Anne** (Wp.6 90M), the abundant vegetation of which seems almost sinfully lavish after the bleak expanse of the sandflats and marsh.

**Digue de la Duchesse Anne**

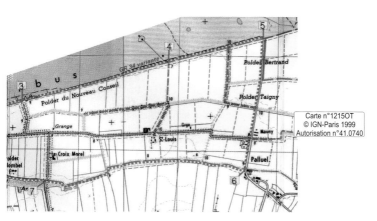

We follow the dike all the way back to the start, crossing a lane 2km short of the chapel (Wp.7 116M), and following another for 650 metres between the **Polder Colombel** and **Ste. Anne** farms (cider for sale).

# 36 LE VERGER: VALLÉES DU ROHUEL & SEREIN

Like many of Brittany's farming communities, the tiny village of **Le Verger**, located midway between **Rennes** and the **Forêt de Paimpont**, has done sterling work waymarking walking and cycling routes, and in this itinerary we explore the neatly coppiced, pastoral landscape surrounding the village, visiting two charming valleys in the process. The route is abundantly, but somewhat confusingly waymarked. Until Wp.17, we follow blue and yellow waymarks, then blue and red, but some care is required between waypoints 20 & 24 as there is no relevant waymarking.

**Access:** on foot from **Le Verger** (accessible by bus from **Paimpont** and **Rennes**).

**Short Version**
Turn left immediately after Wp.20 and follow the waymarks back to **Le Verger**.

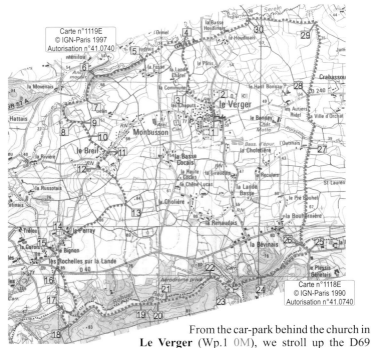

From the car-park behind the church in **Le Verger** (Wp.1 0M), we stroll up the D69 'Route de Talensac' then take the first turning on the left (Wp.2). After passing the entrances to 'Rue des Chênes' and 'Rue des Clos Neufs', we turn right at 'La Commune' on a dirt track lined with chestnut trees (Wp.3 6M). At a T-junction with another track, we bear left, briefly joining the **GR37-A** (yellow & red waymarks, incorrectly mapped by IGN) (Wp.4 12M) as it runs along the shallow **Vallée du Serein**.

75 metres before the hamlet of **La Fosse**, we turn right (Wp.5 18M) on a narrower track shadowing the stream. When the GR swings right to cross a footbridge beside an old millhouse (Wp.6 26M), we carry straight on as indicated by a yellow waymark, staying on the narrow track then forking right at the junction 250 metres later (Wp.7 29M).

The track curves round to the left and we carry straight on at a double junction (Wp.8 35M), following a better stabilized track for 50 metres before turning right on a broad grassy trail (Wp.9). Carrying straight on at the next two junctions (Wp.10 38M), we climb to the hamlet of **Le Breil**, where we briefly join the D240.

Turning right (Wp.11 42M), then left on the 'Le Perray' lane 75 metres later, then left again 50 metres after that (Wp.12), we join a farm track which is surfaced for the first fifty metres. At a crossroads on the crest of a small rise, we turn right (Wp.13 51M), sticking with the main track until it rejoins the lane in Le Perray (Wp.14 59M). Turning left, we follow the lane to 'Le Bignon', then fork left (Wp.15 62M) on a grassy track, at the end of which we cross the D40, bearing slightly left to join another dirt track (Wp.16 65M), signposted 'Les Balcon de Monterfil'. This track descends into the idyllic, densely forested **Vallée du Rohuel**.

Rohuel, near Wp.17

After crossing the stream, we leave the yellow waymarked route and bear left on the blue and red waymarked route (Wp.17 74M). Bearing left again at a staggered crossroads (Wp.18 77M), we continue on a narrower, rougher trail, soon passing a fine outcrop of rock, after which the trail dwindles to a lovely path winding between the mossy trunks of chestnut and oak.

**Fungi in Rohuel (after Wp.18)**

Carrying straight on at a junction with a broad track crossing the valley (Wp.19 89M), we pass a couple of tumbledown cabins with lean-tos sheltering picnic tables (green bottom guaranteed if you use the benches, see picture over the page), 100 metres after which, we come to a junction with the 'Circuit de St. Thurial' (Wp.20 90M), at which point some care is required as the next stage of the walk is <u>not waymarked</u>.

We carry straight on here and once again 30 metres later (the wayposted, blue-waymarked route to the left is a shorter version of our itinerary), then fork left at the next Y-junction (Wp.21 91M).

**Green bottom guaranteed (Wp.19)**

Continuing along the bed of the valley, we ignore numerous trodden ways climbing to the right and a track on the left into an old quarry (Wp.22 100M) before joining the waymarked (blue arrows backed by wheels) trail of a mountain bike itinerary - again, beware!

25 metres after joining the mountain bike itinerary, we <u>leave the waymarked route</u> and double back to the left (Wp.23 104M) on the main track into the quarry. Once in the quarry, we bear right and go to the right of green gates enclosing a reservoir, then follow a trail alongside the reservoir fence, at the end of which we come to a junction of waymarked routes (Wp.24 111M).

Ignoring the yellow waymarked route that climbs to the left, we carry straight on along the reservoir access track, which is surfaced for the last couple of hundred metres before rejoining the D40 (Wp.25). 50 metres to the left (Wp.26 119M), we take a dirt track climbing back onto the agricultural uplands to the east of Le Verger. We now simply follow this track, carrying straight on at each junction, notably that with the **L'Outinais** lane (Wp.27 132M). We then cross the D240 (Wp.28 140M) and turn left 700 metres later at the first crossroads (Wp.29 150M). This track leads to a T-junction, where we bear left (Wp.30 158M), rejoining the GR, which we follow back to Wp.4 (166M).

A lovely woodland stroll amid majestic oak, beech, chestnut and larch interleaved with a pleasant pastoral landscape, and all a mere ten kilometres from the comparatively busy coastal area around the **Rance**. Add an attractive abbey and a spectacular megalithic covered alley and you have the makings of an ideal break from the beach.

**The Abbaye du Tronchet**

Keep your eyes peeled for red squirrels in the heart of the forest. Twitchers should come prepared to twitch and anyone fond of a mushroom should bring their basket in autumn (if in doubt, take the fungi to a chemist for identification). The walk is a variant on the yellow waymarked **Circuit du Forêt du Mesnil**. Except in very dry weather, some mud is to be expected.

2    3H    11.5 km    50m / 50m    2

**Access:** on foot from **Le Tronchet**, which lies between **Dinan** and **Dol-de-Bretagne**.

**Strolls**

There are numerous car-parks and lay-bys giving access to the heart of the forest, notably on the D9 between **Le Tronchet** and **Tressé**.

We set off from the **Abbaye du Tronchet** car-park just north of **Le Tronchet** village, partly because it's a convenient starting point, but also because it's worth strolling round the abbey grounds, above all to admire the spectacular, 300 year-old holly tree in the courtyard.

Carte n°1216O
© IGN-Paris 1998
Autorisation n°41.0740

From the car-park (Wp.1 0M), we follow the D75 back

**Cloisters at the abbey**

to the village. 75 metres after the D75 runs into the D9, we turn left on a lane signposted 'Les Mariais'/'Les Fresches' (Wp.2 10M). We follow this lane past the turning for 'Les Fresches', after which it becomes a dirt track.

After passing two tracks off to the right, we take the third

**The main track from Wp.4**

turning on the right (Wp.3 22M), then carry straight on along the main track 100 metres later (Wp.4) and again at the next, staggered junction (Wp.5 28M). Immediately after crossing the tiny **Pont d'Agou** footbridge (Wp.6 33M), we fork right, following a virtually pathless, waymarked shortcut through the woods to the D73 (Wp.7 36M).

Crossing the road, we head southwest on a broad, slightly monotonous track until the waymarked route doubles back to the right at a signposted triple junction (Wp.8 42M).

At this point, we leave both the main track and the waymarked route, forking right on a minor trail heading northwest. Our trail cuts through the heart of the forest, passing a turning off to the right (Wp.9 49M) before reaching the major, multiple junction known as **Le Jardin d'Amour** (Wp.10 53M). We carry straight on and maintain direction (NW) once again at a long, staggered crossroads (Wp.11 57M).

When the trail reaches a lay-by on the D9 (Wp.12 64M), we follow the road (NW) for 100 metres to the next bend (Wp.13), where we again carry straight on, maintaining a northwesterly direction on a broad grassy track.

**The Roche aux Fées**

Just before the cusp of a tiny rise some 400 metres later, we rejoin the yellow waymarked route, turning left (Wp.14 74M) to reach the megalithic monument known as the **Roche aux Fées** 75 metres later (Wp.15).

We now follow the yellow waymarks for the rest of our itinerary, and very necessary they are too, as the woods here are an absolute tangle of unmapped trails, foragers' paths, and oddly divergent trodden ways.

**Following the necessary yellow waymarks**

Turning right for 'Le Haut Mesnil', we re-cross the approach track and follow the waymarks as they trace out a complicated route meandering through the woods.

The waymarked route forks left, off the main trodden way, after about 150 metres (Wp.16 86M) then bears right at a triple junction just after the first of several footbridges over drainage ditches (Wp.17 89M). Winding through ever denser woodland, we cross another of the major tracks bisecting the forest (Wp.18 95M) and another 100 metres later (Wp.19). After skirting a small marsh and a patch of pond, we turn left on a third broad trail (Wp.20 104M), then right at a junction in a glade 75 metres later (Wp.21) to reach the D73 (Wp.22 113M).

On the other side of the road, a narrow, well maintained path follows a mossy wall into a large field, where it swings right and heads east along the edge of the field, passing behind the rundown but rather magnificent hamlet of **Haut Mesnil**. The path reenters the woodland at the southeastern corner of the field, 50 metres short of a lane (Wp.23 121M). We turn right then, 50 metres later, left on a forestry track for 'Bourg du Tronchet'.

At the first crossroads (Wp.24 127M), we can either turn right to return directly to the village (rejoining the described route at Wp.29) or, as mapped, turn left to visit the **Lac de Mireloup**. 200 metres later (Wp.25), the waymarked route opts for a fork on the right, in fact a mere detour to avoid a stretch of track prone to mud. Otherwise, we simply follow the track until it joins the asphalted access lane above the **Barrage de Mireloup** (Wp.26 137M).

Turning right, we follow the waymarked route (blue diamonds and yellow stripes) as it shadows the lakeshore, though you may wish to ignore the superfluous detour when the waymarked route first cuts into the woods (Wp.27 143M), carrying straight on instead. Eventually, the path feeds into a dirt track just short of a creek.

At the shallow scar of a ditch 150 metres to the southwest, we fork left (Wp.28 156M) and follow either of the two waymarked paths through the woods to join a dirt track on the edge of **St. Malo** golf course (Wp.29 159M). Turning left and immediately forking right, we traverse the golf course, carrying straight on at the next crossroads (Wp.30 164M) before following a minor lane back to the abbey.

# 38 SAINT-MEDARD-SUR-ILLE: LE BOIS DE CRANNE & LE CANAL D'ILLE ET RANCE

The countryside to the north of **Rennes** is comparatively densely populated, absorbing the spill over population from the regional capital while at the same time remaining very much working countryside.

**The Canal d'Ille et Rance**

In this itinerary, we explore the rolling pastoral landscape around **Saint-Medard-sur-Ille**, an attractive village perched above the **Canal d'Ille et Rance**. Built in the early nineteenth century to ensure a secure trading route, the canal cuts across Brittany from the Atlantic to the Channel and runs for 144km, passing 61 locks en route.

The best known stretch is at **Bazouges-sous-Hede**, where an easy stroll visits eleven locks in half as many kilometres, but for a more varied outing, we've opted for the **Sentier du Bois de Cranne** (waymarking plaques No.8), which combines a decent stretch along the canal with pleasant countryside and a lovely wood where one can see deer and even ermine according to one account - the only wildlife we saw was a gracefully ungainly heron.

Our itinerary is one of the **Chemins du Val d'Ille**, all twenty of which are **outlined in a folder of map sheets available at the** Saint-Medard *mairie* for 5 euros. The waymarking only appears at major junctions and is refreshingly discreet: it's nice not to be taken for an orientation imbecile, but some care is required at junctions, since we don't have interminable dots and dashes confirming we're on trail.

**Access:** on foot from **Saint-Medard**, which is served by the railway line between **Rennes**, **St. Malo** and **Dinan**.

**Strolls**
There are countless access points to the canal, ideal for simple tow-path strolls.

We set off from the car-park at the **Saint Medard** lock (*ecluse*) (Wp.1 0M) and follow the asphalted towpath to the north on the western bank of the canal. Ten minutes later, we pass a lock-keeper's cottage, after which the tarmac gives way to grass. The tow path then runs alongside the retaining wall of a railway embankment, where waymarks and a waypost indicate a narrow path off to our left (Wp.2 17M). Bearing left, we climb obliquely through the woods then shadow a cutting before joining a lane beside a railway bridge (Wp.3 22M). We turn left then, 75 metres later, just before the farm, left again (Wp.4) on a muddy track leading to a fieldside right-of-way; if you're walking

**The Saint Medard lock**

with a dog, you may have to duck under the electric fence into the next field; yer actual Breton cow gets a bit frisky when confronted with alien quadrupeds. At the southern end of the field, we go through a gate into another field (Wp.5 32M) and follow a narrow, slightly overgrown path defined by a broken fence to a T-junction (Wp.6 37M) where we turn right to reach the lane through the hamlet of **La Haute** Touche (Wp.7 40M). Turning right, we follow the 'Montreuil-sur-Ille' lane for 250 metres then turn left (beware, the waypost is shrouded by shrubbery) (Wp.8 46M) on a grassy track that immediately dwindles to an attractive path lined with ivy-rimed chestnut and oak.

**The farm near Wp.4**

The path broadens to a dirt track that becomes a surfaced lane after it passes **Le Haut Montmur** farmhouse. At the calvary in the centre of 'Mon Mur' (Wp.9 64M), we turn right (there's an obvious shortcut carrying straight on), staying on tarmac till we reach the hamlet of **Les Landelles**, where we turn left on a track passing in front of the first farmhouse (Wp.10 69M). Behind the farmhouse, the track dwindles to twin trails heading northwest to an unmarked junction with the end of another dirt track (Wp.11 75M). Turning right then left 50 metres later (Wp.12) we pick up another grassy trail defined by tangled hedgerows.

At a T-junction with an unmarked dirt track (Wp.13 84M), we turn left and stroll along an alley of magnificent oaks to reach a divergence of waymarked itineraries at a crossroads with a lane (Wp.14 88M). Ignoring the track to 'La Pommeraie' (Chemins du Val d'Ille N°9), we turn left and follow the lane to the D106 (Wp.15), 300 metres after which, just past the brow of a slight rise, we turn right on a dirt track (Wp.16 102M) (again, there's an obvious shortcut carrying straight on).

When the track joins another lane (Wp.17 107M), we turn left then fork left 75 metres later into the hamlet of **La Rouale** (Wp.18). On the far side of the hamlet, the road feeds into a muddy sunken path leading to the end of a road in La Guéhardière. Turning left (Wp.19 115M) then right at the next crossroads (Wp.20 117M), we pass a farmhouse from where a grassy then muddy track climbs gently toward the **Bois de Cranne**.

At **La Croix Herbelle**, we cross a minor lane (Wp.21 125M) and enter the wood. Ignoring a track curling off to the left in front of a metal gate (Wp.22 130M), we traverse the heart of the wood before descending to a broad track on its southern perimeter, where we turn left (Wp.23 137M).

The track dwindles to a trail, dropping down to a series of footbridges over a diminutive stream where we bear left (Wp.24 143M) following a cow path along the edge of the wood.

The path then re-crosses the stream (Wp.25 151M) and burrows into the densest section of the wood. After turning left at a T-junction in front of green gates (Wp.26 159M), we emerge at the eastern end of the wood (Wp.27 164M), where we turn right and climb to join a lane from **Saint-Germain-sur-Ille** (Wp.28 170M).

Bearing right, we follow the road for 200 metres then fork left (Wp.29) on a driveway leading to a trail descending back to the canal (Wp.30 178M) where we simply turn left to return to the start. Shortly after the second railway bridge, there's an optional, five-minute, signposted detour up to the **Chapelle de Sainte Anne** - very optional given that the thing got bombed along with the railway bridges during the Second World War and was rebuilt in a rather charmless modern idiom: only for the devout and those in dire need of shelter from the elements.

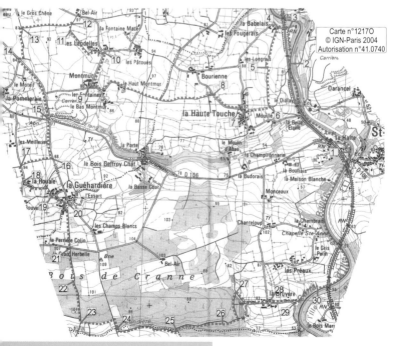

For anyone with an antipathy to straight lines, the great state owned French forests can seem a grim prospect, bisected as they are by grand alleys that look like the work of a man with a very long ruler and very little imagination. Like the formal French garden, the *forêts domaniales* are a kind of Cartesian riposte to the crooked winding ways so beloved by the British. Nonetheless, there is an appeal to these alleys with their magnificent canopies of beech, oak and chestnut, stretching away into the distance, drawing you on, and when you tire of being drawn on, all you need do is duck into the wood and do a bit of weaving between the trees.

There's an infinity of walks to be pieced together in the **Forêt Domaniale de Rennes** and this itinerary is designed to give as broad a picture as possible of what can be done. As a consequence, there are two waymarked off path sections and one unmarked off path section, but in neither instance should pathfinding be a problem. Ideal as a refreshing break after a day doing the culture-vulture/shopaholic stuff in the regional capital, though don't venture onto the off path sections in failing light.

* though **Saint Sulpice la Forêt** just up the road is famous for its restaurants and is a popular weekend retreat for the bourgeoisie of **Rennes**.

**Access:** by car

| **Stroll/Short Version** |
| --- |
| Either of the loops would be a satisfying outing on its own. |

We start in the heart of the forest from the 'Carrefour du Grand Bat' car-park beside the **Etang des Maffrais** on the D528. From the car-park (Wp.1 0M) we stroll up the road to the northwest then, just before the 'Carrefour du Pinçonnais' car park, turn right on a leafy trail burrowing into the woods between the lake and the main **Ligne Forestière de l'Etang** dirt track (Wp.2 4M). This path is part of the **Circuit Pedestre de Saint Sulpice la Forêt**, which we touch upon several times in the westerly halves of our two loops.

There's a maze of diverging ways in the woods here but we stick with the waymarked path (old red and new yellow waymarks), carrying straight on at a crossroads (Wp.3 13M) before the Circuit Pedestre crosses the main *Etang* track (Wp.4 18M). We leave the waymarked route here, turning right and following the track (NE) to the **Carrefour de Boessel** roundabout, where we take the second branch on the right, signposted 'Vers Liffre' (Wp.5 30M). Another straight line, this time southeast leads to an intersection with the **GR39** (Wp.6 36M). Turning right, we follow the GR all the way back to the car park.

After another dead straight stretch, we fork left at a clearly waymarked junction (Wp.7 44M) and wind through the woods, crossing two badly churned up logging tracks (Wp.8 49M). Some care is required here as it's easy to stray off path. Do not follow the tracks but head SSW to join a clear track 50 metres later (Wp.9). Turning left, we head south to a junction with a broad

**Grand alleys**

alley pricked by canalization inspection hatches (Wp.10 55M). Again, some care required. In case you're not familiar with it, the GR waymark bisected by a slanting line is the old waymark meaning 'change direction'. In this instance, we get constant change direction waymarks, since instead of continuing on the main alley, we double back to the right into the woods, OFF PATH, and follow the waymarks through the woods. If in doubt, simple stay on the left of the stream as it meanders back and forth.

Carte n°1218E
© IGN-Paris 2001
Autorisation n°41.0740

After five minutes winding through the woods, we emerge on a clear path 75 metres short of a surfaced track (Wp.11 61M), which we cross onto a clear path alongside a drainage ditch that leads directly back to the car-park (69M).

For the slightly longer southerly loop (6km), we take the main **Maffrais** dirt track to the southwest. 150 metres from the car-park, at a crossroads where the **Parcours Ecologique** turns right, we turn left (Wp.12 71M) on a slightly narrower alley heading southeast. 25 metres short of a lane, we turn right on a broad alley following the interred canalization pipe supplying Rennes with its water (Wp.13 85M). Carrying straight on at the crossroads 500 metres later (Wp.14 92M), we stay with the canalization alley for another 900 metres, until it reaches another surfaced lane (Wp.15 103M).

At this point, we double back to the right (NW) on a narrow, obscure way, essentially off path in places, waymarked with white dots. When the way emerges on a clear, broad trail, we turn right (Wp.16 107M) then right again on the main **Maffrais** track (Wp.17 111M). 150 metres later, we turn left (Wp.18) into a patch of partially cleared woodland choked with saplings and offshoots. Initially, we follow a rough logging trail, but this soon peters out and we again have to make our way essentially off-path, though this time without waymarks. There's no one way, but progress is relatively easy in the tufty grass and before long we emerge on a broad bridleway (Wp.19 121M) just north of a junction with the **Circuit Pedestre de Saint Sulpice**.

We turn right here, though if the bridleway's too muddy, it's possible to follow the waymarked **Saint Sulpice** path through the woods parallel to the main trail. The two trails merge briefly after 350 metres (Wp.20 126M) and again 400 metres later (Wp.21 134M), at which point we fork right and follow the waymarked route along a narrow path, weaving through the woods on the edge of another clearing to join another broad track (Wp.22 138M). We turn right, then left 50 metres later (Wp.23) to join the **Parcours Ecologique** seen at the start of the southerly loop (Wp.24 141M). We can either turn left here or, as mapped, right, in either case, rejoining the main **Maffrais** track (Wp.25 145M) and turning left to return to the car park.

Another *forêt domaniale*, less extensive than that of **Rennes**, but equally beguiling and blessed by a skein of streams and undulating contours that add variety to the itinerary. The woodland paths are (surprise, surprise) particularly lovely in Autumn, but the beaten way can be obscured by the carpet of leaves, so some care is required to follow the waymarked route. Our itinerary combines the **Circuit de la Long Noëe** and **Circuit des Vieux Châteaux**, linking the two by a brief off path shortcut. Other circuits are outlined on a mapboard at the **Carrefour de Chênnedet**.

| 2 | 2½ H | 9.5 km | 50m / 50m | ⟳ | 0 |

**Access:** by car or bus from **Fougères**.

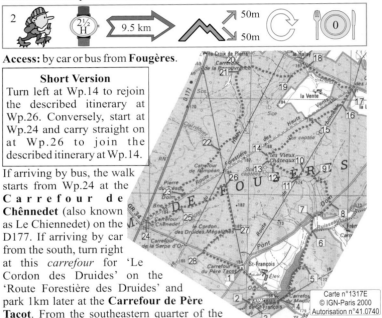

**Short Version**
Turn left at Wp.14 to rejoin the described itinerary at Wp.26. Conversely, start at Wp.24 and carry straight on at Wp.26 to join the described itinerary at Wp.14.

If arriving by bus, the walk starts from Wp.24 at the **Carrefour de Chênnedet** (also known as Le Chiennedet) on the D177. If arriving by car from the south, turn right at this *carrefour* for 'Le Cordon des Druides' on the 'Route Forestière des Druides' and park 1km later at the **Carrefour de Père Tacot**. From the southeastern quarter of the Père Tacot crossroads, we take the **Promenade des Vieux Châteaux** (Wp.1 0M), a waymarked (blue and yellow) path winding through the woods and descending gently between tall beech before crossing two footbridges, the first across a ditch, the second across a stream 75 metres later (Wp.2 6M).

Forking left at a Y-junction (Wp.3 10M) and crossing the access road in front of the 'Moulin St. François' nightclub/leisure centre (Wp.4 13M), we follow the path (not the track) along the eastern shore of the mill lake. Toward the end of the lake, the path contours round a creek, and we turn left to cross a canalization alley (Wp.5 21M). The lake gives way to beech wood framed by fields and we re-cross the stream via another footbridge (Wp.6 28M). When the path joins a minor road, we turn right (Wp.7 30M), then left a couple of hundred metres later (Wp.8 33M), still following the signposted 'Promenade des Vieux Châteaux'.

After crossing another canalization alley (Wp.9 38M), we reach a dirt track (Wp.10 40M), where we turn left, then right 100 metres later (Wp.11) on a narrow path which curves round to the **Vieux Châteaux** themselves, some rather modest defensive earthworks from the pre-Roman period (Wp.12 47M). At this point, we leave the **Circuit des Vieux Châteaux**. 50 metres to the right, slightly to the left of the head of the broad trail fronting the dikes, a faint way (Wp.13) heads northwest between densely packed saplings before entering mature woodland again and joining the **Circuit de la Long Noëe** (Wp.14 50M). Wp.26 lies 400 metres to the southwest, but we turn right here and follow the pinkish waymarks to the northeast.

Carrying straight on at a crossroads with a cycle itinerary (Wp.15 60M) then bearing left on a major dirt track (**Route de la Cherbonnelais**) (Wp.16 64M), we reach the **Carrefour des Hauts Vents** near the northern perimeter of the forest. Crossing the private road doubling back to the left, we turn left on a path signposted 'Promenade de la Long Noëe' (Wp.17 67M).

The path runs parallel to the road, then drops down to cross a footbridge (Wp.18 74M), beyond which we follow both pink and yellow waymarks. After climbing back into the woods, we cross another footbridge and a dirt track (Wp.19 76M). The path divides immediately after the track and we carry straight on (the right hand fork), crossing another track a couple of hundred metres later (poor GPS reception here, hence no waypoint). On the fringes of **Landéan**, we come to a waymarked junction (Wp.20 86M), where we fork left, crossing a waymarked bridleway 100 metres later (Wp.21 87M). Sticking with the pink waymarks, we climb a short flight of steps and cross a clearing, beyond which we re-enter the woods. Reaching a slightly obscure stretch beside a metal post with a pink waymark, we maintain a SW direction, crossing another footbridge 50 metres later (Wp.22 102M). The waymarking becomes a bit erratic as we approach the confluence of the **Route Forestière des Hauts Vents** dirt track and the D177. We can either stay in the woods between the track and the road until we reach the **Carrefour de Chênnedet** or follow the obvious trail onto the track and turn right (Wp.23 111M).

Either way, once back at the **Carrefour de Chênnedet**, we double back to the left on the **Circuit de la Long Noëe** path heading northeast (Wp.24 118M). After forking right at a Y-junction (directly accessible from Wp.23) (Wp.25 124M), we wind through deepening woodland to reach a major dirt track (Wp.26 132M), where we turn right, rejoining the **Promenade des Vieux Châteaux** 500 metres later (Wp.27 138M). We can either carry straight on here to return directly to the start or turn right to follow the *promenade* along the line of the **Cordon des Druides**, a megalithic alignment of eighty odd stones.

**Cordon des Druides**

Presuming you follow the promenade, once past the megaliths, we rejoin the **Route Forestière des Druides**, where we ignore the waymarked route to the south and simply turn left (Wp.28 144M) to stroll through the woods beside of the road (both sides are feasible), off path but guided by the obvious line of the tarmac.

See the notes on GPS use and waypoints on page 16.
Waypoints are quoted for the WGS84 Datum with UTM grid coordinates.

## 1 PLOUGONVELIN

| Wp | EAST | NORTH |
|----|------|-------|
| 01 | 373883 | 5355238 |
| 02 | 373355 | 5355320 |
| 03 | 373026 | 5355190 |
| 04 | 372544 | 5355028 |
| 05 | 372502 | 5355106 |
| 06 | 371827 | 5355063 |
| 07 | 371531 | 5355035 |
| 08 | 371232 | 5355243 |
| 09 | 370898 | 5355245 |
| 10 | 370222 | 5355025 |
| 11 | 370169 | 5354869 |
| 12 | 369797 | 5354760 |
| 13 | 369550 | 5354735 |
| 14 | 369574 | 5354512 |
| 15 | 369607 | 5354344 |
| 16 | 368983 | 5354372 |
| 17 | 368865 | 5354458 |
| 18 | 368569 | 5354566 |
| 19 | 370702 | 5354634 |
| 20 | 371368 | 5354827 |
| 21 | 371787 | 5354569 |
| 22 | 373008 | 5354637 |
| 23 | 373324 | 5354894 |
| 24 | 373298 | 5355049 |

## 2 TRÉZIEN

| Wp | EAST | NORTH |
|----|------|-------|
| 01 | 369230 | 5364872 |
| 02 | 369113 | 5364995 |
| 03 | 369123 | 5365108 |
| 04 | 368617 | 5365189 |
| 05 | 368632 | 5365401 |
| 06 | 368568 | 5365453 |
| 07 | 368099 | 5365617 |
| 08 | 367801 | 5364981 |
| 09 | 367752 | 5364757 |
| 10 | 367555 | 5364666 |
| 11 | 367468 | 5364242 |
| 12 | 367274 | 5363979 |
| 13 | 367506 | 5363669 |
| 14 | 367594 | 5363566 |
| 15 | 368046 | 5363151 |
| 16 | 368513 | 5363179 |
| 17 | 368614 | 5363318 |
| 18 | 368784 | 5363290 |
| 19 | 369229 | 5363992 |
| 20 | 369087 | 5364722 |
| 21 | 369252 | 5364737 |

## 3 PORTSALL

| Wp | EAST | NORTH |
|----|------|-------|
| 01 | 374592 | 5379387 |
| 02 | 374460 | 5379223 |
| 03 | 374405 | 5379103 |
| 04 | 374271 | 5378953 |
| 05 | 374364 | 5378689 |
| 06 | 374554 | 5378696 |
| 07 | 373700 | 5378629 |
| 08 | 372763 | 5377840 |
| 09 | 372740 | 5377690 |
| 10 | 372430 | 5377132 |
| 11 | 372136 | 5376867 |
| 12 | 371959 | 5376633 |
| 13 | 371788 | 5376530 |
| 14 | 371145 | 5376208 |
| 15 | 371326 | 5376376 |
| 16 | 371124 | 5376537 |
| 17 | 371124 | 5376551 |
| 18 | 371025 | 5376688 |
| 19 | 370888 | 5376681 |
| 20 | 371916 | 5378836 |
| 21 | 373290 | 5379824 |
| 22 | 373244 | 5379681 |
| 23 | 373328 | 5379464 |
| 24 | 373636 | 5379244 |
| 25 | 373881 | 5379085 |
| 26 | 374135 | 5378896 |

## 4 GUISSENY

| Wp | EAST | NORTH |
|----|------|-------|
| 01 | 395742 | 5388151 |
| 02 | 395693 | 5387892 |
| 03 | 395378 | 5387578 |
| 04 | 395208 | 5387351 |
| 05 | 395225 | 5387187 |
| 06 | 394945 | 5387104 |
| 07 | 395045 | 5386849 |
| 08 | 395161 | 5386613 |
| 09 | 394760 | 5386088 |
| 10 | 394590 | 5386094 |
| 11 | 394259 | 5386296 |
| 12 | 394058 | 5386279 |
| 13 | 394038 | 5386520 |
| 14 | 393795 | 5386405 |
| 15 | 393303 | 5386501 |
| 16 | 392989 | 5386573 |
| 17 | 392882 | 5386654 |
| 18 | 392893 | 5386888 |
| 19 | 392935 | 5387169 |
| 20 | 392497 | 5387083 |
| 21 | 392421 | 5387154 |
| 22 | 392908 | 5387805 |
| 23 | 393212 | 5388074 |
| 24 | 393896 | 5388194 |
| 25 | 394514 | 5387908 |

## 5 GOULVEN

| Wp | EAST | NORTH |
|----|------|-------|
| 01 | 404202 | 5387107 |
| 02 | 404164 | 5387358 |
| 03 | 404026 | 5387955 |
| 04 | 404036 | 5387476 |
| 05 | 404436 | 5387415 |
| 06 | 404727 | 5388004 |
| 07 | 405007 | 5387955 |
| 08 | 405766 | 5388082 |
| 09 | 405719 | 5388454 |
| 10 | 405873 | 5388588 |
| 11 | 406340 | 5389134 |
| 12 | 407081 | 5389264 |
| 13 | 407288 | 5389192 |
| 14 | 408080 | 5389016 |
| 15 | 408345 | 5389115 |
| 16 | 409026 | 5389345 |
| 17 | 409821 | 5389813 |
| 18 | 408311 | 5389230 |
| 19 | 408058 | 5389193 |
| 20 | 405404 | 5388343 |
| 21 | 404695 | 5388212 |

## 6 MOGUÉRIEC

| Wp | EAST | NORTH |
|----|------|-------|
| 01 | 420636 | 5393470 |
| 02 | 420809 | 5393323 |
| 03 | 421258 | 5393280 |
| 04 | 421518 | 5393119 |
| 05 | 421765 | 5392652 |
| 06 | 421772 | 5392525 |
| 07 | 422044 | 5392131 |
| 08 | 422294 | 5391603 |
| 09 | 422346 | 5391217 |
| 10 | 422487 | 5391168 |
| 11 | 422523 | 5391082 |
| 12 | 422226 | 5390877 |
| 13 | 422143 | 5390759 |
| 14 | 422021 | 5390423 |
| 15 | 422207 | 5390189 |
| 16 | 422560 | 5390127 |
| 17 | 422698 | 5390511 |
| 18 | 422179 | 5391163 |
| 19 | 422053 | 5391634 |
| 20 | 421678 | 5392173 |
| 21 | 421313 | 5392604 |
| 22 | 421132 | 5392814 |

## 7 SANTEC

| Wp | EAST | NORTH |
|----|------|-------|
| 01 | 424846 | 5395831 |
| 02 | 425178 | 5395857 |
| 03 | 425042 | 5395492 |
| 04 | 424889 | 5395366 |
| 05 | 425158 | 5395075 |
| 06 | 424988 | 5394830 |
| 07 | 425439 | 5394627 |
| 08 | 425392 | 5394314 |
| 09 | 425286 | 5394176 |
| 10 | 424470 | 5393851 |
| 11 | 423933 | 5394061 |
| 12 | 423862 | 5393997 |
| 13 | 423544 | 5394048 |
| 14 | 423210 | 5393956 |
| 15 | 423217 | 5393687 |
| 16 | 423216 | 5393480 |
| 17 | 423063 | 5393383 |
| 18 | 422206 | 5393567 |
| 19 | 422276 | 5393957 |
| 20 | 422294 | 5394778 |
| 21 | 422559 | 5394929 |
| 22 | 422597 | 5395057 |
| 23 | 422617 | 5395149 |
| 24 | 422765 | 5395128 |
| 25 | 423291 | 5394928 |
| 26 | 423859 | 5396085 |
| 27 | 423964 | 5396074 |

## 8 CARANTEC

| Wp | EAST | NORTH |
|----|------|-------|
| 01 | 432033 | 5391554 |
| 02 | 431925 | 5391692 |
| 03 | 431786 | 5392188 |
| 04 | 431808 | 5392443 |
| 05 | 431924 | 5392960 |
| 06 | 431852 | 5393489 |
| 07 | 431964 | 5393646 |
| 08 | 431942 | 5394318 |
| 09 | 431999 | 5392331 |

## 9 LE DIBEN TO TERENEZ

| Wp | EAST | NORTH |
|----|------|-------|
| 01 | 438846 | 5395652 |
| 02 | 438905 | 5395470 |
| 03 | 439041 | 5395287 |
| 04 | 439035 | 5395165 |
| 05 | 439034 | 5395059 |
| 06 | 438967 | 5395033 |
| 07 | 438860 | 5394922 |
| 08 | 438836 | 5394751 |
| 09 | 438842 | 5394631 |
| 10 | 438793 | 5394620 |
| 11 | 438825 | 5394434 |
| 12 | 438396 | 5394394 |
| 13 | 438309 | 5394373 |
| 14 | 438189 | 5394343 |
| 15 | 438175 | 5394086 |
| 16 | 438205 | 5393541 |
| 17 | 437781 | 5393651 |
| 18 | 437732 | 5393100 |
| 19 | 437966 | 5392496 |
| 20 | 438021 | 5392340 |
| 21 | 437950 | 5392103 |
| 22 | 437831 | 5391948 |
| 23 | 437616 | 5392048 |
| 24 | 437471 | 5392026 |
| 25 | 437265 | 5392739 |
| 26 | 437480 | 5393663 |
| 27 | 438112 | 5395030 |
| 28 | 438674 | 5395519 |

## 10 PLOUGASNOU

| Wp | EAST | NORTH |
|----|------|-------|
| 01 | 441752 | 5393976 |
| 02 | 442190 | 5393930 |
| 03 | 442601 | 5393799 |
| 04 | 442887 | 5393837 |
| 05 | 443050 | 5393732 |
| 06 | 443100 | 5393638 |
| 07 | 443375 | 5393242 |
| 08 | 443282 | 5393175 |
| 09 | 443285 | 5393065 |
| 10 | 443406 | 5392861 |
| 11 | 443497 | 5392740 |
| 12 | 443739 | 5392592 |
| 13 | 443843 | 5392370 |
| 14 | 443882 | 5391887 |
| 15 | 444164 | 5391817 |
| 16 | 444168 | 5391984 |
| 17 | 444189 | 5392317 |
| 18 | 444335 | 5392395 |
| 19 | 444282 | 5392561 |
| 20 | 444657 | 5392676 |
| 21 | 444648 | 5392748 |
| 22 | 444288 | 5393149 |

| Wp | EAST | NORTH |
|----|------|-------|
| 23 | 444746 | 5393617 |
| 24 | 445592 | 5393351 |
| 25 | 446122 | 5393052 |
| 26 | 446178 | 5392274 |
| 27 | 447511 | 5392347 |
| 28 | 447629 | 5392284 |
| 29 | 447695 | 5392424 |
| 30 | 447785 | 5392399 |
| 31 | 448236 | 5392509 |
| 32 | 448434 | 5393168 |
| 33 | 448226 | 5393181 |
| 34 | 447131 | 5394535 |
| 35 | 447090 | 5394756 |
| 36 | 445953 | 5395261 |
| 37 | 445078 | 5395162 |
| 38 | 444236 | 5395332 |
| 39 | 443536 | 5395170 |
| 40 | 443092 | 5395021 |

## 11 CRANOU

| Wp | EAST | NORTH |
|----|------|-------|
| 01 | 418136 | 5353166 |
| 02 | 418319 | 5353061 |
| 03 | 418685 | 5353035 |
| 04 | 419165 | 5352900 |
| 05 | 419487 | 5353032 |
| 06 | 420672 | 5352574 |
| 07 | 420886 | 5352527 |
| 08 | 421385 | 5352706 |
| 09 | 421802 | 5352742 |
| 10 | 422029 | 5352850 |
| 11 | 421952 | 5352671 |
| 12 | 421845 | 5352578 |
| 13 | 421587 | 5352349 |
| 14 | 421470 | 5352268 |
| 15 | 421240 | 5351801 |
| 16 | 420902 | 5352003 |
| 17 | 420826 | 5352004 |
| 18 | 420662 | 5351682 |
| 19 | 420084 | 5351881 |
| 20 | 418767 | 5351937 |
| 21 | 418714 | 5351922 |
| 22 | 418707 | 5352070 |
| 23 | 418236 | 5352551 |
| 24 | 418224 | 5352699 |

## 12 DRENNEC

| Wp | EAST | NORTH |
|----|------|-------|
| 01 | 424706 | 5360426 |
| 02 | 425062 | 5361320 |
| 03 | 425525 | 5360800 |
| 04 | 425743 | 5360925 |
| 05 | 426116 | 5360858 |
| 06 | 426106 | 5360724 |
| 07 | 426006 | 5360513 |
| 08 | 426399 | 5360656 |
| 09 | 426561 | 5360526 |
| 10 | 426569 | 5360276 |
| 11 | 426847 | 5360109 |
| 12 | 427177 | 5360000 |
| 13 | 426963 | 5360619 |
| 14 | 427250 | 5360871 |
| 15 | 427666 | 5360270 |
| 16 | 427998 | 5360711 |
| 17 | 428255 | 5360956 |
| 18 | 428464 | 5361190 |
| 19 | 428713 | 5360634 |

| Wp | EAST | NORTH |
|----|------|-------|
| 20 | 428591 | 5360577 |
| 21 | 428750 | 5360409 |
| 22 | 428989 | 5359850 |
| 23 | 427564 | 5359452 |
| 24 | 427340 | 5359373 |
| 25 | 427149 | 5359013 |
| 26 | 426954 | 5358753 |
| 27 | 426700 | 5359078 |
| 28 | 426642 | 5359418 |
| 29 | 426038 | 5359758 |
| 30 | 425557 | 5359928 |
| 31 | 425403 | 5359698 |
| 32 | 425067 | 5359915 |

## 13 BRENNILIS

| Wp | EAST | NORTH |
|----|------|-------|
| 01 | 435037 | 5356093 |
| 02 | 434690 | 5356313 |
| 03 | 434880 | 5356556 |
| 04 | 435078 | 5357230 |
| 05 | 434855 | 5357544 |
| 06 | 434308 | 5357553 |
| 07 | 433966 | 5358269 |
| 08 | 432704 | 5357986 |
| 09 | 432369 | 5358055 |
| 10 | 431653 | 5357962 |
| 11 | 431266 | 5359221 |
| 12 | 430425 | 5358557 |
| 13 | 430116 | 5359214 |
| 14 | 430142 | 5359317 |
| 15 | 429462 | 5358190 |
| 16 | 429237 | 5357629 |
| 17 | 429211 | 5357448 |
| 18 | 428784 | 5356370 |
| 19 | 429257 | 5356035 |
| 20 | 429932 | 5355652 |
| 21 | 430104 | 5355477 |
| 22 | 430263 | 5355285 |
| 23 | 430587 | 5354932 |
| 24 | 431329 | 5355011 |
| 25 | 431460 | 5355472 |
| 26 | 431963 | 5355286 |
| 27 | 433452 | 5354754 |
| 28 | 433907 | 5354698 |
| 29 | 435300 | 5355046 |
| 30 | 435998 | 5355957 |
| 31 | 435791 | 5356670 |
| 32 | 435701 | 5356910 |

## 14 CLOÎTRE ST. THÉGONNEC

| Wp | EAST | NORTH |
|----|------|-------|
| 01 | 439715 | 5368116 |
| 02 | 439260 | 5367746 |
| 03 | 439726 | 5367509 |
| 04 | 440154 | 5367117 |
| 05 | 440215 | 5366422 |
| 06 | 439989 | 5365375 |
| 07 | 440071 | 5365173 |
| 08 | 440206 | 5365236 |
| 09 | 440629 | 5365406 |
| 10 | 440966 | 5365522 |
| 11 | 441204 | 5365617 |
| 12 | 441936 | 5366044 |
| 13 | 442015 | 5366071 |
| 14 | 442405 | 5366687 |
| 15 | 442553 | 5366907 |
| 16 | 442637 | 5366760 |
| 17 | 442854 | 5367093 |
| 18 | 442877 | 5367464 |
| 19 | 442640 | 5367422 |
| 20 | 442613 | 5367354 |
| 21 | 442108 | 5367295 |
| 22 | 441810 | 5367097 |
| 23 | 441753 | 5367175 |
| 24 | 441650 | 5367433 |
| 25 | 440379 | 5368271 |
| 26 | 440212 | 5368150 |

## 15 HUELGOAT

| Wp | EAST | NORTH |
|----|------|-------|
| 01 | 445648 | 5357345 |
| 02 | 445489 | 5357763 |
| 03 | 445676 | 5358047 |
| 04 | 445569 | 5358517 |
| 05 | 445689 | 5358670 |
| 06 | 445758 | 5358842 |
| 07 | 445929 | 5359300 |
| 08 | 446193 | 5359562 |
| 09 | 445925 | 5359491 |
| 10 | 445908 | 5359788 |
| 11 | 445873 | 5359816 |
| 12 | 445753 | 5359816 |
| 13 | 445545 | 5360015 |
| 14 | 445318 | 5360230 |
| 15 | 445563 | 5360435 |
| 16 | 445810 | 5360613 |
| 17 | 446071 | 5360980 |
| 18 | 446607 | 5361150 |
| 19 | 446744 | 5360989 |
| 20 | 447391 | 5358946 |
| 21 | 447379 | 5358672 |
| 22 | 447064 | 5357762 |
| 23 | 446645 | 5357411 |
| 24 | 446586 | 5357445 |
| 25 | 446489 | 5357469 |

## 16 HUELGOAT REGAINED

| Wp | EAST | NORTH |
|----|------|-------|
| 01 | 444921 | 5357054 |
| 02 | 445023 | 5356959 |
| 03 | 445034 | 5357053 |
| 04 | 445360 | 5357139 |
| 05 | 445559 | 5357038 |
| 06 | 445732 | 5356533 |
| 07 | 446197 | 5356436 |
| 08 | 446345 | 5356459 |
| 09 | 446497 | 5356337 |
| 10 | 446485 | 5356628 |
| 11 | 446535 | 5356951 |
| 12 | 446269 | 5356733 |
| 13 | 445940 | 5356914 |
| 14 | 445919 | 5357051 |
| 15 | 445663 | 5357339 |
| 16 | 445498 | 5357758 |
| 17 | 445199 | 5358381 |
| 18 | 444949 | 5358546 |
| 19 | 444818 | 5358535 |
| 20 | 444901 | 5358345 |
| 21 | 444990 | 5358078 |
| 22 | 445448 | 5357400 |
| 23 | 444905 | 5357329 |

## 17 GUERLESQUIN

| Wp | EAST | NORTH |
|----|------|-------|
| 01 | 456597 | 5373958 |
| 02 | 456897 | 5373941 |
| 03 | 457219 | 5373963 |
| 04 | 457544 | 5373893 |
| 05 | 457531 | 5373514 |
| 06 | 457143 | 5372508 |
| 07 | 456963 | 5372430 |
| 08 | 456550 | 5372222 |
| 09 | 456649 | 5371522 |
| 10 | 456212 | 5371223 |
| 11 | 456320 | 5371036 |
| 12 | 456022 | 5370920 |
| 13 | 455810 | 5371061 |
| 14 | 455535 | 5371699 |
| 15 | 454957 | 5371838 |
| 16 | 455016 | 5372348 |
| 17 | 455168 | 5372612 |
| 18 | 455008 | 5372769 |
| 19 | 454506 | 5373016 |
| 20 | 454266 | 5373182 |
| 21 | 454084 | 5373831 |
| 22 | 454086 | 5373894 |
| 23 | 454038 | 5374295 |
| 24 | 454150 | 5374439 |
| 25 | 454219 | 5374623 |
| 26 | 454399 | 5374696 |
| 27 | 454698 | 5374553 |
| 28 | 455033 | 5374236 |
| 29 | 455163 | 5374058 |
| 30 | 455963 | 5374053 |

## 18 TRÉDREZ-LOQUÉMEAU

| Wp | EAST | NORTH |
|----|------|-------|
| 01 | 457403 | 5396857 |
| 02 | 457260 | 5396608 |
| 03 | 457026 | 5396152 |
| 04 | 457110 | 5396216 |
| 05 | 457575 | 5395824 |
| 06 | 457673 | 5395301 |
| 07 | 457738 | 5394756 |
| 08 | 457808 | 5394662 |
| 09 | 458117 | 5394281 |
| 10 | 458252 | 5394165 |
| 11 | 458268 | 5393972 |
| 12 | 458200 | 5393412 |
| 13 | 458018 | 5393388 |
| 14 | 457754 | 5393335 |
| 15 | 457746 | 5393580 |
| 16 | 457556 | 5393575 |
| 17 | 457374 | 5393131 |
| 18 | 457225 | 5393107 |
| 19 | 457246 | 5393665 |
| 20 | 457291 | 5394776 |
| 21 | 457277 | 5395342 |

## 19 PLOUMANAC'H

| Wp | EAST | NORTH |
|----|------|-------|
| 01 | 466173 | 5407228 |
| 02 | 466149 | 5407403 |
| 03 | 465605 | 5407932 |
| 04 | 465627 | 5407757 |
| 05 | 465459 | 5407554 |
| 06 | 465425 | 5407417 |
| 07 | 465165 | 5407310 |
| 08 | 465059 | 5407207 |
| 09 | 465095 | 5407078 |
| 10 | 464645 | 5407106 |
| 11 | 464461 | 5407722 |
| 12 | 464135 | 5407820 |
| 13 | 464154 | 5408051 |
| 14 | 464138 | 5408669 |
| 15 | 463997 | 5408652 |
| 16 | 464303 | 5409091 |
| 17 | 464562 | 5409391 |
| 18 | 464777 | 5409390 |
| 19 | 465265 | 5408619 |

## 20 PLOUGRESCANT

| Wp | EAST | NORTH |
|----|------|-------|
| 01 | 480756 | 5409138 |
| 02 | 480953 | 5409006 |
| 03 | 481217 | 5408772 |
| 04 | 481465 | 5408724 |
| 05 | 481279 | 5408519 |
| 06 | 481792 | 5408358 |
| 07 | 481949 | 5408132 |
| 08 | 482393 | 5408455 |
| 09 | 482496 | 5408562 |
| 10 | 482763 | 5408448 |
| 11 | 482790 | 5408229 |
| 12 | 482942 | 5408257 |
| 13 | 482922 | 5408423 |
| 14 | 483434 | 5408082 |
| 15 | 483697 | 5408336 |
| 16 | 483944 | 5408573 |
| 17 | 483935 | 5408981 |
| 18 | 484507 | 5410700 |
| 19 | 484478 | 5411152 |
| 20 | 484291 | 5411615 |
| 21 | 483932 | 5412090 |
| 22 | 483902 | 5412590 |
| 23 | 483558 | 5412730 |
| 24 | 483419 | 5412831 |
| 25 | 483000 | 5412657 |
| 26 | 482835 | 5412550 |
| 27 | 482923 | 5412386 |
| 28 | 482527 | 5411925 |
| 29 | 482147 | 5411756 |
| 30 | 481800 | 5411115 |
| 31 | 481601 | 5410804 |
| 32 | 481298 | 5410111 |
| 33 | 481090 | 5409679 |

## 21 LEZARDRIEUX

| Wp | EAST | NORTH |
|----|------|-------|
| 01 | 493051 | 5402839 |
| 02 | 493124 | 5402936 |
| 03 | 493083 | 5403267 |
| 04 | 493212 | 5403853 |
| 05 | 493323 | 5403956 |
| 06 | 493184 | 5404277 |
| 07 | 493186 | 5404479 |
| 08 | 493431 | 5405129 |
| 09 | 493643 | 5405513 |
| 10 | 493896 | 5406644 |
| 11 | 494384 | 5407051 |
| 12 | 494569 | 5407222 |
| 13 | 494768 | 5407403 |
| 14 | 495145 | 5407625 |
| 15 | 495041 | 5407021 |
| 16 | 494899 | 5406633 |
| 17 | 494545 | 5406692 |
| 18 | 494463 | 5406320 |
| 19 | 494334 | 5406385 |
| 20 | 494206 | 5406108 |
| 21 | 494324 | 5405974 |
| 22 | 494082 | 5405885 |
| 23 | 494242 | 5405586 |
| 24 | 494319 | 5405332 |
| 25 | 493721 | 5404920 |
| 26 | 493481 | 5404788 |
| 27 | 493430 | 5404455 |

## 22 PORDIC

| Wp | EAST | NORTH |
|----|------|-------|
| 01 | 515352 | 5380744 |
| 02 | 515593 | 5380054 |
| 03 | 515433 | 5379817 |
| 04 | 515283 | 5379564 |
| 05 | 515526 | 5379462 |
| 06 | 516341 | 5379445 |
| 07 | 516704 | 5379577 |
| 08 | 516329 | 5380320 |
| 09 | 516237 | 5380708 |
| 10 | 515731 | 5381195 |
| 11 | 514843 | 5381462 |
| 12 | 514386 | 5381866 |
| 13 | 514173 | 5382064 |
| 14 | 514311 | 5381820 |
| 15 | 514345 | 5381501 |
| 16 | 514573 | 5381289 |
| 17 | 514690 | 5381272 |
| 18 | 514813 | 5381146 |

## 23 HILLION

| Wp | EAST | NORTH |
|----|------|-------|
| 01 | 524444 | 5373472 |
| 02 | 524876 | 5373416 |
| 03 | 526055 | 5373190 |
| 04 | 526181 | 5373347 |
| 05 | 526754 | 5373528 |
| 06 | 527092 | 5373538 |
| 07 | 527139 | 5374046 |
| 08 | 527276 | 5373993 |
| 09 | 527361 | 5374285 |
| 10 | 526721 | 5374556 |
| 11 | 525712 | 5374530 |
| 12 | 525441 | 5374536 |
| 13 | 525197 | 5374744 |
| 14 | 524862 | 5375388 |
| 15 | 524400 | 5375857 |
| 16 | 523519 | 5375516 |
| 17 | 523748 | 5374555 |
| 18 | 523959 | 5373774 |
| 19 | 523978 | 5373461 |

## 24 ERQUY

| Wp | EAST | NORTH |
|----|------|-------|
| 01 | 539469 | 5386329 |
| 02 | 539658 | 5386268 |
| 03 | 540024 | 5386391 |
| 04 | 540548 | 5386487 |
| 05 | 541730 | 5386754 |
| 06 | 541789 | 5386777 |
| 07 | 542117 | 5386850 |
| 08 | 542662 | 5386907 |
| 09 | 542972 | 5387209 |
| 10 | 542648 | 5388332 |
| 11 | 542072 | 5388570 |
| 12 | 541610 | 5388845 |
| 13 | 540981 | 5388726 |
| 14 | 540626 | 5388514 |
| 15 | 540219 | 5388402 |
| 16 | 540142 | 5388313 |
| 17 | 539819 | 5388401 |
| 18 | 539505 | 5388337 |
| 19 | 538979 | 5388239 |
| 20 | 538860 | 5388075 |
| 21 | 538602 | 5387871 |
| 22 | 538132 | 5387963 |
| 23 | 537850 | 5388100 |
| 24 | 538021 | 5387806 |
| 25 | 538180 | 5387560 |
| 26 | 538189 | 5387426 |
| 27 | 538482 | 5387290 |
| 28 | 538481 | 5387350 |
| 29 | 538789 | 5387306 |
| 30 | 539172 | 5387552 |
| 31 | 539243 | 5387265 |

## 25 CAP FRÉHEL & FORT LA LATTE

| Wp | EAST | NORTH |
|----|------|-------|
| 01 | 552026 | 5390378 |
| 02 | 551831 | 5390321 |
| 03 | 551520 | 5390360 |
| 04 | 551137 | 5389917 |
| 05 | 550983 | 5390017 |
| 06 | 550869 | 5390285 |
| 07 | 550643 | 5390687 |
| 08 | 550546 | 5390669 |
| 09 | 550229 | 5390608 |
| 10 | 549860 | 5390465 |
| 11 | 549662 | 5390357 |
| 12 | 549255 | 5391033 |
| 13 | 549561 | 5391576 |
| 14 | 549738 | 5392106 |
| 15 | 550243 | 5392755 |
| 16 | 550415 | 5391743 |
| 17 | 551084 | 5390814 |
| 18 | 552471 | 5390677 |
| 19 | 552501 | 5390248 |
| 20 | 552070 | 5390124 |

## 26 ST. JACUT-DE-LA-MER

| Wp | EAST | NORTH |
|----|------|-------|
| 01 | 558402 | 5380314 |
| 02 | 558605 | 5380568 |
| 03 | 558639 | 5380690 |
| 04 | 558928 | 5381234 |
| 05 | 559079 | 5381640 |
| 06 | 559333 | 5382069 |
| 07 | 559595 | 5382396 |
| 08 | 559607 | 5382168 |
| 09 | 559930 | 5382173 |
| 10 | 560047 | 5382615 |
| 11 | 560093 | 5382750 |
| 12 | 560321 | 5383091 |
| 13 | 559314 | 5384556 |
| 14 | 559578 | 5385750 |
| 15 | 559847 | 5386260 |
| 16 | 559785 | 5386101 |
| 17 | 559390 | 5383373 |
| 18 | 559520 | 5382928 |

## 27 BELLE-ISLE-EN-TERRE

| Wp | EAST | NORTH |
|----|------|-------|
| 01 | 470789 | 5377075 |
| 02 | 470719 | 5377241 |
| 03 | 470665 | 5377414 |
| 04 | 470735 | 5377583 |
| 05 | 470570 | 5378045 |
| 06 | 470580 | 5378487 |
| 07 | 470664 | 5378461 |
| 08 | 470713 | 5378695 |
| 09 | 470183 | 5378985 |
| 10 | 469691 | 5379653 |
| 11 | 469441 | 5379711 |
| 12 | 469188 | 5379565 |
| 13 | 469547 | 5379112 |
| 14 | 469731 | 5378800 |
| 15 | 470114 | 5378192 |

## 28 SAINT NICODÈEME

| Wp | EAST | NORTH |
|----|------|-------|
| 01 | 472774 | 5353426 |
| 02 | 472327 | 5353346 |
| 03 | 471523 | 5353994 |
| 04 | 471467 | 5354202 |
| 05 | 471449 | 5354281 |
| 06 | 471322 | 5354505 |
| 07 | 471766 | 5354625 |
| 08 | 472050 | 5354623 |

## 29 TREMARGAT

| Wp | EAST | NORTH |
|----|------|-------|
| 01 | 480149 | 5353295 |
| 02 | 479723 | 5353654 |
| 03 | 478572 | 5352969 |
| 04 | 478304 | 5353395 |
| 05 | 478225 | 5353527 |
| 06 | 478406 | 5354287 |
| 07 | 478585 | 5354770 |
| 08 | 478666 | 5355407 |
| 09 | 479038 | 5355467 |
| 10 | 479708 | 5355187 |
| 11 | 479857 | 5355034 |
| 12 | 480424 | 5355073 |
| 13 | 480673 | 5354961 |
| 14 | 480962 | 5354855 |
| 15 | 481328 | 5354676 |
| 16 | 481404 | 5354274 |
| 17 | 481666 | 5354196 |
| 18 | 481737 | 5353696 |
| 19 | 481828 | 5353375 |
| 20 | 481854 | 5353336 |
| 21 | 481967 | 5353086 |
| 22 | 481974 | 5352749 |
| 23 | 482041 | 5352559 |
| 24 | 481745 | 5352937 |
| 25 | 481499 | 5353416 |
| 26 | 481368 | 5353602 |
| 27 | 481215 | 5353739 |
| 28 | 480936 | 5352677 |
| 35 | 495798 | 5339639 |
| 36 | 495053 | 5339341 |
| 37 | 495044 | 5339466 |
| 38 | 495280 | 5339593 |
| 39 | 495053 | 5340065 |
| 40 | 494629 | 5340318 |
| 41 | 494216 | 5340232 |
| 42 | 494062 | 5340105 |
| 43 | 493874 | 5340099 |
| 44 | 493830 | 5339789 |
| 45 | 493600 | 5339934 |
| 46 | 493244 | 5339977 |
| 47 | 492826 | 5340074 |
| 48 | 491818 | 5339943 |
| 49 | 491832 | 5339371 |

## 30 MUR-DE-BRETAGNE

| Wp | EAST | NORTH |
|----|------|-------|
| 01 | 490468 | 5340014 |
| 02 | 490489 | 5340213 |
| 03 | 490431 | 5340323 |
| 04 | 491164 | 5340355 |
| 05 | 491877 | 5340046 |
| 06 | 492056 | 5340049 |
| 07 | 492321 | 5340265 |
| 07 | 493595 | 5340517 |
| 09 | 493834 | 5340631 |
| 10 | 494336 | 5340573 |
| 11 | 495168 | 5340247 |
| 12 | 495438 | 5340222 |
| 13 | 496430 | 5340269 |
| 14 | 496628 | 5340186 |
| 15 | 497044 | 5340254 |
| 16 | 497686 | 5340239 |
| 17 | 498441 | 5340249 |
| 18 | 498848 | 5340181 |
| 19 | 498877 | 5340045 |
| 20 | 498652 | 5339984 |
| 21 | 498078 | 5339662 |
| 22 | 498352 | 5339411 |
| 23 | 498542 | 5338734 |
| 24 | 498741 | 5338447 |
| 25 | 498316 | 5338385 |
| 26 | 498249 | 5338452 |
| 27 | 497908 | 5338494 |
| 28 | 497608 | 5338913 |
| 29 | 497502 | 5338992 |
| 30 | 497160 | 5339160 |
| 31 | 496821 | 5339239 |
| 32 | 496993 | 5339649 |
| 33 | 496323 | 5339734 |
| 34 | 495994 | 5339601 |

## 31 PLOUFRAGAN

| Wp | EAST | NORTH |
|----|------|-------|
| 01 | 511766 | 5370721 |
| 02 | 511545 | 5370635 |
| 03 | 511660 | 5369723 |
| 04 | 511608 | 5368911 |
| 05 | 511074 | 5368552 |
| 06 | 511220 | 5368275 |
| 07 | 512319 | 5367251 |
| 08 | 512361 | 5367182 |
| 09 | 512404 | 5367059 |
| 10 | 512827 | 5366681 |
| 11 | 512630 | 5366466 |
| 12 | 512260 | 5366366 |
| 13 | 512336 | 5365934 |
| 14 | 512013 | 5365808 |
| 15 | 511774 | 5365399 |
| 16 | 511974 | 5364757 |
| 17 | 511844 | 5365030 |
| 18 | 511848 | 5365549 |
| 19 | 512393 | 5367157 |
| 20 | 512420 | 5367497 |
| 21 | 512388 | 5367587 |
| 22 | 512203 | 5368161 |
| 23 | 511822 | 5368820 |
| 24 | 511977 | 5369978 |

## 32 LANGAST

| Wp | EAST | NORTH |
|----|------|-------|
| 01 | 525267 | 5347285 |
| 02 | 525458 | 5347227 |
| 03 | 525296 | 5346656 |
| 04 | 525339 | 5346513 |
| 05 | 525310 | 5346334 |
| 06 | 525612 | 5346174 |
| 07 | 525818 | 5346059 |
| 08 | 525982 | 5346129 |
| 09 | 526169 | 5345800 |
| 10 | 526197 | 5345470 |
| 11 | 526135 | 5345395 |
| 12 | 525921 | 5345336 |
| 13 | 526256 | 5345072 |
| 14 | 526335 | 5344190 |
| 15 | 526443 | 5344165 |
| 16 | 526514 | 5343906 |
| 17 | 526197 | 5343862 |
| 18 | 525876 | 5344065 |
| 19 | 525959 | 5344544 |
| 20 | 525582 | 5345140 |
| 21 | 525431 | 5345056 |
| 22 | 525339 | 5345264 |
| 23 | 525827 | 5345415 |
| 24 | 525508 | 5347265 |

## 33 JUGON LES LACS

| Wp | EAST | NORTH |
|----|------|-------|
| 01 | 549501 | 5365378 |
| 02 | 548874 | 5365334 |
| 03 | 549060 | 5365578 |
| 04 | 549060 | 5365899 |
| 05 | 549750 | 5366200 |
| 06 | 549555 | 5367037 |
| 07 | 550146 | 5367354 |
| 08 | 550353 | 5367407 |
| 09 | 549773 | 5366745 |
| 10 | 549487 | 5365936 |
| 11 | 549586 | 5365197 |

## 34 CANCALE

| Wp | EAST | NORTH |
|----|------|-------|
| 01 | 584456 | 5394305 |
| 02 | 584354 | 5394324 |
| 03 | 584188 | 5394074 |
| 04 | 583922 | 5394077 |
| 05 | 583480 | 5394010 |
| 06 | 583059 | 5394101 |
| 07 | 582838 | 5394110 |
| 08 | 582843 | 5393967 |
| 09 | 582856 | 5393910 |
| 10 | 582361 | 5393840 |
| 11 | 581831 | 5394013 |
| 12 | 581601 | 5394346 |
| 13 | 582054 | 5394320 |
| 14 | 583007 | 5394378 |
| 15 | 583713 | 5394624 |
| 16 | 584225 | 5395418 |
| 17 | 584989 | 5395790 |
| 18 | 585003 | 5395600 |
| 19 | 584576 | 5394788 |
| 20 | 584713 | 5394248 |
| 21 | 584667 | 5394256 |

## 35 CHERRUEIX

| Wp | EAST | NORTH |
|----|------|-------|
| 01 | 598009 | 5385047 |
| 02 | 599347 | 5385217 |
| 03 | 600421 | 5385514 |
| 04 | 601897 | 5385930 |
| 05 | 602850 | 5386197 |
| 06 | 602695 | 5384828 |
| 07 | 600680 | 5384676 |

## 36 LE VERGER

| Wp | EAST | NORTH |
|----|------|-------|
| 01 | 579517 | 5324622 |
| 02 | 579516 | 5324760 |
| 03 | 579276 | 5324910 |
| 04 | 579224 | 5325356 |
| 05 | 578839 | 5325234 |
| 06 | 578341 | 5325068 |
| 07 | 578259 | 5324829 |
| 08 | 578143 | 5324593 |
| 09 | 578213 | 5324584 |
| 10 | 578304 | 5324409 |
| 11 | 578472 | 5324277 |
| 12 | 578369 | 5324112 |
| 13 | 578659 | 5323751 |
| 14 | 578112 | 5323426 |
| 15 | 577960 | 5323247 |
| 16 | 578015 | 5323045 |
| 17 | 578057 | 5322633 |
| 18 | 578104 | 5322449 |
| 19 | 578832 | 5322700 |
| 20 | 578993 | 5322707 |
| 21 | 579067 | 5322731 |
| 22 | 579507 | 5322959 |
| 23 | 579684 | 5322849 |
| 24 | 580026 | 5323004 |
| 25 | 580504 | 5323281 |
| 26 | 580436 | 5323340 |
| 27 | 580490 | 5324321 |
| 28 | 580486 | 5324857 |
| 29 | 580548 | 5325620 |
| 30 | 579881 | 5325656 |

## 37 LE TRONCHET

| Wp | EAST | NORTH |
|----|------|-------|
| 01 | 586071 | 5371506 |
| 02 | 585915 | 5371008 |
| 03 | 586475 | 5370372 |
| 04 | 586426 | 5370240 |
| 05 | 586145 | 5370118 |
| 06 | 585775 | 5369834 |
| 07 | 585591 | 5369735 |
| 08 | 585167 | 5369524 |
| 09 | 584649 | 5369845 |
| 10 | 584398 | 5370015 |
| 11 | 584110 | 5370193 |
| 12 | 583633 | 5370515 |
| 13 | 583478 | 5370613 |
| 14 | 583098 | 5370860 |
| 15 | 583007 | 5370792 |
| 16 | 583140 | 5371059 |
| 17 | 583244 | 5371224 |
| 18 | 583640 | 5371330 |
| 19 | 583725 | 5371405 |
| 20 | 584069 | 5371431 |
| 21 | 583957 | 5371600 |
| 22 | 584274 | 5371838 |
| 23 | 584765 | 5371893 |
| 24 | 585099 | 5371861 |
| 25 | 584997 | 5372066 |
| 26 | 584783 | 5372514 |
| 27 | 585098 | 5372308 |
| 28 | 585299 | 5371763 |
| 29 | 585315 | 5371502 |
| 30 | 585509 | 5371360 |

## 38 SAINT-MEDARD-SUR-ILLE

| Wp | EAST | NORTH |
|----|------|-------|
| 01 | 599076 | 5347533 |
| 02 | 598446 | 5348440 |
| 03 | 598399 | 5348788 |
| 04 | 598309 | 5348815 |
| 05 | 598229 | 5348384 |
| 06 | 598242 | 5347994 |
| 07 | 597995 | 5347931 |
| 08 | 597678 | 5348095 |
| 09 | 596417 | 5348149 |
| 10 | 596547 | 5348519 |
| 11 | 596228 | 5348716 |
| 12 | 596228 | 5348787 |
| 13 | 595730 | 5348736 |
| 14 | 595717 | 5348409 |
| 15 | 596030 | 5347802 |
| 16 | 596072 | 5347392 |
| 17 | 595756 | 5347318 |
| 18 | 595793 | 5347188 |
| 19 | 596068 | 5347015 |
| 20 | 596213 | 5346950 |
| 21 | 596276 | 5346494 |
| 22 | 596332 | 5346154 |
| 23 | 596410 | 5345710 |
| 24 | 596767 | 5345662 |
| 25 | 597381 | 5345668 |
| 26 | 597805 | 5345719 |
| 27 | 597968 | 5346067 |
| 28 | 598296 | 5345974 |
| 29 | 598541 | 5345984 |
| 30 | 598760 | 5346126 |

## 39 RENNES

| Wp | EAST | NORTH |
|----|------|-------|
| 01 | 607417 | 5340659 |
| 02 | 607189 | 5340809 |
| 03 | 607611 | 5341318 |
| 04 | 607636 | 5341618 |
| 05 | 608101 | 5342332 |
| 06 | 608449 | 5342040 |
| 07 | 608222 | 5341528 |
| 08 | 608272 | 5341148 |
| 09 | 608247 | 5341090 |
| 10 | 608340 | 5340739 |
| 11 | 608077 | 5340766 |
| 12 | 607242 | 5340466 |
| 13 | 607625 | 5339908 |
| 14 | 607183 | 5339572 |
| 15 | 606743 | 5338831 |
| 16 | 606498 | 5338972 |
| 17 | 606247 | 5339164 |
| 18 | 606310 | 5339241 |
| 19 | 605887 | 5339390 |
| 20 | 606138 | 5339695 |
| 21 | 606417 | 5340085 |
| 22 | 606676 | 5340268 |
| 23 | 606727 | 5340205 |
| 24 | 606817 | 5340311 |
| 25 | 606980 | 5340124 |

## 40 FOUGÈRES

| Wp | EAST | NORTH |
|----|------|-------|
| 01 | 636951 | 5361218 |
| 02 | 637018 | 5360885 |
| 03 | 637146 | 5360833 |
| 04 | 637344 | 5360907 |
| 05 | 637581 | 5361259 |
| 06 | 637642 | 5361635 |
| 07 | 637647 | 5361791 |
| 08 | 637813 | 5361914 |
| 09 | 637659 | 5362205 |
| 10 | 637547 | 5362283 |
| 11 | 637485 | 5362187 |
| 12 | 637229 | 5362297 |
| 13 | 637173 | 5362342 |
| 14 | 637165 | 5362416 |
| 15 | 637657 | 5362780 |
| 16 | 637901 | 5362939 |
| 17 | 638009 | 5363133 |
| 18 | 637558 | 5363336 |
| 19 | 637397 | 5363232 |
| 20 | 636903 | 5363322 |
| 21 | 636881 | 5363270 |
| 22 | 636700 | 5362436 |
| 23 | 636355 | 5362005 |
| 24 | 635965 | 5361686 |
| 25 | 636330 | 5361865 |
| 26 | 636767 | 5362108 |
| 27 | 636868 | 5361636 |
| 28 | 636562 | 5361400 |